OTHER BOOKS FROM TRUEFACE

 The Cure

 Bo's Café

 The Ascent of a Leader

 Behind the Mask

 On My Worst Day

 Lay It Down

BILL & GRACE **THRALL**   JOHN & STACEY **LYNCH**   BRUCE & JANET **McNICOL**

THE
CURE
& PARENTS

FOREWORD BY DAVID & KELSIE PINKERTON

Printed in the USA
First Edition: October 2016

Published by Trueface
1730 E Northern Ave Ste 106
Phoenix, AZ 85020
602-249-7000

ISBN 978-1-934104-09-5

CONTENTS

FOREWORD

We are, truth be told, not at all famous. Most people think we are supposed to be at least a little famous when writing a foreword, especially for a book that we absolutely hope everyone we know—and more importantly those we don't know—will read.

Why did we want to write this? Because this message has saved our lives and given us such practical hope in enjoying the insanity of raising our kids. Because we are the parents of three precocious and opinionated littles (eight, six, and four) as Kelsie runs a busy wedding photography business and David works fulltime with Trueface, all while giving as much time as possible to the high school students and others at our church. And because we are normal people with a very vivid picture of what we'd like our relationships with our children to look like (and not look like) as they grow older, but often have no idea how to achieve the reality of these dreams in the moments when things are hard.

Why should you listen to a couple that works with the authors of a parenting book? Because we have been in close community with the authors of this book long enough (more than ten years) to put the principles of the original gospel to the test. We have watched from the front row as these couples have imperfectly but faithfully carried these truths into their own homes with their own children and grandchildren, most of whom we have relationships with today. In this community, we have tasted the freedom that comes from having the worst known about us and being loved more for it. We have felt poison in us dissipate by experiencing the miracles of forgiveness and restoration. We have experienced breakthroughs in our marriage and relationships that we couldn't have conjured on our own. We have watched some of our generational patterns be broken in such a way that our children will never have to know them.

In short, we have seen and experienced grace, the original good news of Jesus in action. And it works. It is the only thing that works. We believe it has the capability to bring freedom to every parent, single parent, grandparent, soon-to-be parent, young adult pondering his or her family of origin, or person who is in any way involved in caring for another person's life.

As soon as we finished the first draft, we knew we wanted to put *The Cure and Parents* in the hands of every person we know and love. If you are fairly normal, or even if you are kinda famous, read this, and find practical powerful hope that will help you realize the trusted joyful relationship you have always dreamed of with your kids.

With you on this journey,
David and Kelsie Pinkerton

INTRODUCTION

Some parenting books are written to buy time until your kids get old enough to reason with you.

This is not that book.

Some are written to help you get your kids on board, fix their attitudes, and compel them to behave better.

This is not that book.

Some are designed to help keep your kids from embarrassing you in public.

This is not that book.

Some are filled with techniques and formulas so you can gain the upper hand in battles with your kids.

This is most certainly not that book.

This book is much more about *us*—the parents.

There is a cruel joke that somehow slipped in under the door. It goes like this:

> *These children we waited and longed for have now become our opponents. Opponents we love, but ones we now have to manage.*

It's not supposed to be this way. God gave us children to enjoy endlessly, and for them to be able to enjoy us for an entire lifetime.

That's why we wrote this book. To learn how to earn our children's trust so we can receive the wonderfully transformative privilege of

- ♦ giving our children love,
- ♦ teaching them truth, and
- ♦ providing them guidance.

When we discover the truth of this next statement, nearly everything begins to change in the way we parent:

> *Because God's primary goal is earning my trust so He can love me and increasingly mature me, correct my behavior, and free my life, I will attempt to offer the same for my child.*

God has done endlessly more than enough to have earned my trust. But He knows that until I actually, *practically* trust Him, very little He desires for me will come to pass. *My lack of trust comes from my fear of trust, not His worthiness to be trusted.* So, because He loves me so deeply, He continually reveals Himself as trustworthy, breaking down my fears and walls of self-preservation. And as I grow to trust the Perfectly Trustworthy One, I heal, I mature, I become free.

It's why David called out, "Oh, taste and see that the Lord is good!" (Psalm 34:8, ESV). He was saying, "When you are able to see Him accurately and trust His intentions for you, oh, what a marvelous life you will have with Him!"

So this has been God's means for my maturity all along. And as I begin to understand it for me, it becomes the means for me to help my children mature.

Maturity and lasting behavior change do not happen by coercion or technique—in my children or in me.

I can have very little meaningful impact upon my children until they begin to trust my influence.

I can give them knowledge. I can offer them information. To some extent, especially when they are younger, I may even be able to leverage their behaviors.

But little of that brings meaningful, life-transforming influence.

Until I believe this, I will be tempted to parent by technique-driven formulas, to effect something that looks like change in my children.

We have so much more to offer them.

We get to give our kids the best of us—earning permission to influence them, mature them, know them, give guidance to them,

IV

protect them, love them, free them, and show them a magnificent God and an authentic life that will hold up for their entire lifetime.

We get to authentically and vulnerably know them. They get to watch us trusting God. They watch us mature and heal and become freer. They experience us growing to trust them with our issues. They get to enjoy, instead of maneuvering around, the very ones who have loved them most.

We get to leave an indelible relational mark they won't want to ever shake.

This is where we're heading, and a story will take us there.

We will be riding along with the Clawsons on their vacation. In many ways, the Clawsons are us. They face many of the same parenting issues we face. We will watch them interact, hear them process with God, even catch snippets of podcasts, all with the goal of integrating this way of living into our day-to-day experience.

You'll notice that, instead of chapters, this book is filled with episodes. After each episode, we're offering a look "Inside the Episode." This is where we (the authors) will unpack some of the truths and challenges presented in the Clawsons' story. And just so you know, this book is designed as a companion to *The Cure: What If God Isn't Who You Think He Is and Neither Are You?* In that book, we lay all the theological foundation needed for the Clawsons' story. You don't have to read that book to "get" this one. We see them not as two sides of the same coin as much as dance partners. We feel they perform quite beautifully together.

Parents, far from something to endure until your kids finally leave the house, we believe parenting can be the trip of a lifetime.

So, friends, enjoy the ride.

MEET THE PARENTS

Silence is golden. Until it isn't.

No one in the car is talking. No one's been talking the seventy-five miles stretching from North Phoenix to the first rest area on the way to Los Angeles. Only the dull hum of tires on the interstate. Everyone except the driver has those little white ear buds in, all intentionally listening to anything but each other. Jim Clawson is the driver. He's the dad.

And he is also much of the reason no one is talking to each other.

Jim and his wife, Sarah, occupy the front seats while fourteen-year-old Madison and nine-year-old Aiden sit in the back. At this moment, they're only resentful passengers in a crowded vehicle. As Jim turns the car off, ear buds are removed. And for just a moment, before everyone climbs out, there is a very *ungolden* silence. It is whispering to each of the Clawsons that something is very wrong with their family.

This was supposed to be an epic vacation. Something in it for everyone. Out of the withering Arizona summer heat, for several days at Newport Beach. Then up the coast to Monterey and San

Francisco, finally circling back home through several national parks.

Supposed to be. Ah, what a phrase.

Now all Jim can see is a frustrated wife, an angry daughter, and a son who wears mismatched clothes for no reason except, apparently, to exasperate his parents.

It's never easy to know the exact moment when a family begins to find itself. It may be easier to pinpoint when things got darkest. For the Clawsons, that particular moment might have been last evening.

Maybe they should have seen it coming. Some of the worst blowups a family can experience are in the two- to three-day window before the start of a family vacation, or on the way to church on Sunday morning. Surely this is documented somewhere. Surely.

Last evening, just after dinner, Madison, halfway out of the front door, had called, "Going to Jeff's."

Three little words.

Jim Clawson is not fond of this Jeff. He is not particularly fond of any fifteen-year-old boy.

He ran out into the front yard, yelling loudly enough for neighbors to hear, "You're not going anywhere. Your room is a mess, you're not packed, and there are things your mom has asked you to do that you still haven't done. Oh, and we've never even yet met this Jeff." Madison was no more than twenty feet from Jim. His yelling was clearly for effect.

She was humiliated, hurt, and angry. Then hurt and angry. Then only angry. All within seconds. She turned and ran past him back into the house and slammed the door to her bedroom. Jim followed after her, pounding hard on her locked door.

"Why do you always do this? Madison, open the door!"

Silence.

"I don't want you seeing that boy. Do you hear me?"

More silence.

"Do you hear me!"

The door violently swung open. Madison stepped back and slowly spit out these words: "I'm not deaf. Neither is the whole neighborhood. I get it—you don't trust me. You don't trust any of us. Oh, and I never wanted to go on this stupid vacation. So I'll be as miserable as I possibly can. Watch me."

She timed these last words with the slamming of the door.

It is now fifteen hours later at this barren desert rest stop. Jim, Sarah, Madison, and Aiden each climb back into their fully packed Subaru Forrester, each one slamming a door.

Long before this trip, Sarah had stumbled across a parenting podcast series a friend had highly recommended titled "Enjoy the Ride." She downloaded the series onto her phone. Her plan was to play segments of it along the road each day, to pass the time and maybe involve the kids in some way. Jim was surprisingly open to it.

Now the idea seems ridiculous. And manipulative.

Approaching Blythe, California, the desert sameness is taking its toll on all of them.

"Dad, make Aiden move away from me."

"Jim, I hate the desert."

"Sarah, I should have filled up the tank back in Phoenix."

"Mom, did someone wash my shirt in vomit? It smells like vomit."

Blythe, in the middle of summer, can make any issue worse. They follow the Lovekin off-ramp onto a street devoted almost entirely to fast-food restaurants. It is early afternoon on July 14—116 degrees, on its way to 118. As they walk from the car to this vacation's first meal, the parking lot asphalt is actually spongy.

Once in the car, sharing burgers, tacos, and onion rings causes multiple arguments. And Madison is complaining to Jim that the AC is not getting to her.

"It's still not aimed at the back seat," she says in a loud sigh.

"I already adjusted the vent."

"It's aimed at your door. Nobody's sitting there. I'm back here. In the back seat."

"Then your mom and I won't have air on us."

"You have other vents. For example, the one aimed at the door."

And so on.

Jim, gamely trying to change the mood, asks, "Let's listen to that podcast."

Madison puts her ear buds back in. Aiden does the same.

"Jim, I don't think that's a good idea right now."

"Sarah, the last thing I want to listen to is a parenting podcast. But there are no good radio stations out here. And I'm the only one without ear buds."

3

"Do what you like. But not me. Maybe later."

"But I need your phone to play it."

"Then how am I supposed to listen to my music?"

"C'mon, Sarah. Just play it for ten minutes."

As the Clawsons pull onto the on-ramp, heading west on Interstate 10, the first session of "Enjoy the Ride" begins.

The narrator's rich alto voice fills the already crowded Subaru. Her first words are startling:

> *"When your children are young, being the parent carries enough control to handle them. But if you don't grow up as they grow older, your immaturity will stunt their maturity at the level of your own. And no measure of control can handle that."*

Almost involuntarily, Jim and Sarah do what they've been avoiding the last seventeen hours. They look at each other.

"Wait. What did she just say?"

"What?" Jim responds, still stunned by the narrator's words.

"The woman on the podcast. What did she just say?"

Jim sneaks a glance into the rear view mirror to see if Madison or Aiden are listening. They are both staring out into the desert on either side of the car, ear buds firmly in place.

Sarah pauses the audio.

"Something about my immaturity, I think. Can you play it back?"

She does.

> *"But if you don't grow up as they grow older, your immaturity will stunt their maturity at the level of your own. And no measure of control can handle that."*

"So what's that supposed to mean?" Sarah pauses the podcast.

"I have no idea. It's your podcast."

Several miles go by.

Sarah, almost to herself, says, "When they were younger, it wasn't so complicated. I just had to be okay with them destroying the sugar packets in restaurants. And the crying. And the lack of sleep. And cleaning sand out of everything. It was nonstop. But I usually thought I knew what I was doing. Now Madison gives me this look that says, 'You have no clue what to do with me right now, do you?'"

Jim is listening, but careful not to respond.

"And she's absolutely right. She's on to me. I have no clue how to parent her anymore."

Several more miles pass by. The road fifty yards ahead looks like a lake in the heat-formed mirage of midday.

"I'm becoming who I promised myself I would never be. All the things I would never say. All the rules I told myself I'd never impose on my kids. The manipulation, the control, fighting on their level. And now … I'm doing it."

Somewhere near Chiriaco Summit, Sarah turns the podcast back on.

And they just let it play. All the way through the first session.

Both look into the back seat at their now sleeping kids.

Jim and Sarah gradually begin talking to each other. It is neither personal nor animated. But it is talking. Not silence.

INSIDE THE EPISODE

We begin with the quote that stopped Jim and Sarah in their collective tracks:

> *"When your children are young, being the parent carries enough control to handle them. But if you don't grow up as they grow older, your immaturity will stunt their maturity at the level of your own. And no measure of control can handle that."*

Parenting exposes unresolved issues we might otherwise ignore or be perpetually unaware of. Like it or not, those we love tend to most often reveal unresolved issues in us.

An "unresolved issue" is a significantly recurring problem that increasingly affects our lives because it never gets better.

These issues embarrass us, so it's easy to cover them over and hope they go away. But they don't. Instead, they're "buried alive," erupting when we are overstressed, challenged, enflamed, wronged, or insecure.

If anything is to change, we must admit that some things have happened in our lives that, well, just shouldn't have happened. And we've been harmed by what happened. For many, it is too costly to admit this. So we learn to limp around our wounds. Gradually, we learn to cover up or clean up the symptoms so our issue won't embarrass us. Or we try to ignore it, hoping it will just go away over time.

It doesn't.

Many of us can go a lifetime almost oblivious to this baggage we carry. Sadly, we may be the only ones oblivious to this. Most others can see it, though they may not be sure what they're seeing.

Here's the deal. You know you are carrying around an unresolved issue when you are told by more than one key person in your life that you are overreacting to a situation. This overreacting is the result of wounding. You can usually trace that wounding back to three things: your own sin, someone else's sin against you, or someone important to you consistently choosing to not love you.

Unless our wounding is identified and addressed so it can be redeemed and healed, we will remain with an unresolved issue, stunted in our immaturity. And our children will be stunted in their immaturity by ours, with the ongoing result of our children not trusting us.

Trust is developed as our kids begin to believe we have the maturity not to make something about us when they need it to be about them.

And their trusting us is dependent on our trusting God with who He says we are and allowing Him to redeem and heal us from our wounding and unresolved issues.

So how do we bring, and keep bringing, an unresolved issue into the light where it can no longer rob our children of our best?

Well, strap in. Here we go.

Many of us might think what Jesus did on the cross accomplished only heaven for us. Initial rightness with God. The doorway to new life. All that is endlessly and astonishingly true. But that same cross provides a means for current, present-tense healing and cleansing, and a way home from unresolved issues!

Trusting in Christ's long-ago cross releases a profound power that can cleanse me today and begin the process of healing from my unresolved sins.

At the cross, God and I were forever made right with each other once and for all. None of that has to be revisited. But that same payment is actively working for me in whatever stuff is plaguing my heart and soul.

So, I can stop trusting in my willpower to fix me and my unresolvedness. I choose instead to trust that what Jesus did back then frees me from the effects of sin in me right here and now.

This trusting isn't voodoo or an immediate fix. But it is the starting point for all healing. It changes the chemistry of the equation. It levels the playing field so I can grow in maturity and freedom. It resets my heart. All so I can bring my stuff into the light and not hold onto it in the darkness, hoping it will go away.

My only job, at least for the moment, is to believe that, in this instant, the cross has power to cleanse me and release me from my present experience of guilt, shame, and any lesser identity than Christ in me.

That's it? Yeah, that's kind of it. And the word used to describe this entire process? Redemption.

This is the stunning beginning of our parenting journey. It sounds like make-believe—too good to be true. But it is as real as anything we can see. Without trusting this redemption, we are stuck with our own failed abilities to solve, clean, and heal ourselves. And that has never worked for any of us.

We don't have to have it all figured out or know the right words to say. We just have to believe God has the power to cleanse us and start healing us from the power of our particular issue.

And we don't have to beat ourselves up if we don't feel much different at first. Like good medicine, redemption is taking place even before we feel its effects.

That's a lot, right? It's probably wise to stop here and let the last few paragraphs sink in.

There are really very few wrong initial reactions to this—unless you blow past this section, pretending you can stand with your kids in their life issues before you've faced your own, or even worse, pretending you already "get it."

So it occurs to us this might be the time to give some deeply needed hope. Facing unresolved life issues can sound pretty daunting. And it may dredge up some historic shame.

Shame. That nagging voice trying to tell you that you are not enough, that you will never be enough. That there is something about you uniquely and permanently stained with darkness, strangeness, and failure.

This entire book is undergirded, surrounded, based upon, and empowered by a word that describes so much more than a concept or mere theology. Five letters that can change everything—grace—the totally undeserved favor, love, complete acceptance and delight of God. It is the gift of inexhaustible love to humans who never saw it coming. It pierces our deepest historic shame and declares, "I know. And I'm not leaving. I'm crazy about you."

- ♦ You are absolutely right on time.
- ♦ You are completely enough to be the parent of your children.
- ♦ He cannot love you more than He does and He will never love you less.
- ♦ He has made you righteous, holy, and without condemnation for every step of this journey.
- ♦ God loves you to the exact extent that He loves His only Son.
- ♦ You are never being played by God.
- ♦ God never sees you as endlessly behind, unable to catch up.
- ♦ He is not ashamed of you or ever disgusted with you.
- ♦ You fully belong.
- ♦ You are fully enough.
- ♦ You have a brand-new, shame-free identity.

He has recreated you with a new nature, a new story. You are never who your shame might try to declare. You are not your shame. This is how all heaven sees you.

Quite frankly, grace changes everything.

It is enough right now to tell you that grace reveals a God who is not against you, but endlessly for you. A God who is never disgusted or angry with you. He planned for there to be a "you" even before the world began. He has great plans for your life. You are completely enough to be the parent of your children. And whatever you think you can never be healed of, please, please think again.

We just thought you might need to be reminded of that.

E PISODE
TWO

UNDER NEW MANAGEMENT

I t's late afternoon and the Clawsons cross the bridge over Highway 1 onto Newport Boulevard toward Oceanfront. Crossing that bridge is the moment vacation traditionally starts for this family. At B Street they turn down a familiar tiny alley leading to Sarah's parents' beach house garage. Most years, for two weeks in July, this condo directly facing the Pacific Ocean is their home. And their last chance to find each other again before another school year ramps up.

The hour of unpacking and moving in is usually filled with music and excited, happy yelling to each other from all over the condo. But after the last twenty-four hours, this all suddenly feels like a dull task. What's usually a memory-filled safe place feels more like an impersonal motel. There's very little conversation. Mostly only the sound of drawers opening and closing. Aiden is the first to finish. He runs out to the water. Sarah follows after him at a distance. Madison walks out onto the bike path toward Balboa pier. Jim goes to the second floor balcony and sits.

By the time Jim gets settled in his chair, Aiden is already digging in wet sand. Aiden could happily stay all vacation in the ten-yard circle around him. Sarah stares out toward the horizon as the California sun begins to melt into the ocean.

Sarah is pondering the differences between her kids. Aiden is the anti-Madison. The compliant one. He rarely gets into trouble and does what he's told. But Sarah wonders if maybe Aiden is just checking out. Maybe it's just a way to game the system in his favor. Keeping the peace may just be a way to buy more uninterrupted iPad time.

Sarah remembers a statement from the parenting podcast about compliant kids. She fiddles with her phone to find the exact place in the podcast so she can hear the words again.

"Early on, rules are essential to parenting and protecting our children. But as they grow older, rules need to be merged and eventually replaced with principles that will help guide them. But if we haven't learned principles, we may resort to imposing more rules onto our children because it feels like we're able to better control their behaviors. And we will discover we have raised either rebellious or compliant children. But such compliant children do not mature well as they grow older. And as they age, they can hold you responsible for their failed life choices."

"Great," Sarah whispers. "That's just great. I think we've managed to raise both types."

The podcast continues:

"Compliant children don't get to learn how to own their life choices. In an environment where parents only impose rules through their child's adolescence, it can thwart and stunt them from learning to own their choices. So a compliant, immature child grows into a compliant, immature young adult. When they discover imposed life choices didn't work, they have no one to hold responsible but their parents."

Sarah's unfocused stare moves to Aiden. He has not looked up at her, or anyone, since he reached the water. He's alone in his own imaginary world.

No one is nearby. She finds herself praying out loud: "Am I doing that to my son? Teaching him to comply? Maybe I just got tired fighting Madison. I thought I was doing it right with Aiden. Thought if we didn't fight, I'd be a good parent. But I've just been wearing him down. 'When will you? Why haven't you? Get in here! Hurry up! Don't do that! Do this! Why are you so…?' He's shutting down. He stays quiet now for so long. Same stuff I forced onto Madison. It's just that she fought back."

The sun has set.

"I don't know how to parent them. Jim thinks he does. But he's too much for them. He can't see it. He thinks parenting is fixing them, getting them to shape up. To make them good citizens, or something."

Sarah repeatedly scoops up sand and lets it run through her fingers.

"It seems so natural for other moms. Like they were cut out for it from birth. It doesn't come easy for me. I've let Jim do the heavy lifting. And now I resent him for how he does it. Help me, God. Help us. Don't let us fall apart. I don't know what I'm asking. I just don't want to lose them. I don't want to screw this all up."

INSIDE THE EPISODE

We're at a crossroads here. We can take the low road of trading relational life for what promises to fix our kids and us. We may choose the external fixes because we are afraid. We know the issues we struggled with growing up and we truly want to stop our kids before they have to experience that pain and failure. But the "fix" creates an unforeseen consequence often worse than the issue it was brought in to fix. Sarah has gotten in touch with this form of parenting that has helped her feel more in control. But the unforeseen consequence is a growing disengagement with her children's hearts.

"Sin management" is the misguided presumption that we're supposed to figure out how to master our own bad behavior. Or the behavior of others. And until we can, we are to fake it and give the appearance of maturity. The sin management mindset usually starts with the crippling theological conviction that, while we may be saved, we are only saved sinners. Not yet really saints. While perhaps sincere, this theological construct is ultimately immensely destructive. We strive hard to please God by our better behaviors but have little dependence or trust in anything more than self-abnegating willpower, sincerity, and a wavering ability to say no.

This is the oldest and most dangerous false approach to healing and maturing. But to be fair, it has been heaped on us in a thousand ways. Our entire culture tells us to be self-reliant and pull ourselves up by our bootstraps. In addition to that, many of us in Christian cultures are fairly certain that we are most often a disappointment to God. And to others. So we keep desperately trying to be good enough while convinced we never will be. We resemble the dog chasing his tail.

Sadly, this bogus logic has infected so many of our churches. And such warped theology is not easily abandoned unless we're convinced there is a better way. And we can end up imposing this broken system on our own children. But God has given us a better motivation for our children than just staying out of trouble. A better reason to do right than "because I told you so." A better way to teach them heartfelt obedience instead of an external compliance. God has given us the most excellent on-ramp to their hearts—that of love.

Engendering heartfelt obedience takes more time. But compliance will leave us with anesthetized, presentable-looking teenagers who will adopt a very different lifestyle once they leave our home.

To understand a way home from compliance, we must begin to understand how God has created us to move from rules to guidelines.

In children's early development, rules are a profound and wonderful protection. Rules protect their hearts and give them a way of safely interacting with their world. But without a plan to gradually release them to discover guidelines and principles, rules alone become a destructive life pattern and an inadequate motivation for life.

As children grow and mature, guidelines must begin to replace rules.

A rule is a directive or prohibition aimed at governing a specific behavior. It is inflexible and comes with a direct penalty if violated. Early on, it can give healthy protection and boundaries for children before they can morally reason through wrong and right, dangerous and safe behavior. Rules are a great gift from the Father. They never go completely off the screen in our lives. Businesses, government, and societies always work best with rules and laws in place.

But the human heart needs much more. And much less.

Over time, if rules are all we use to parent, our kids can learn a resentful response of begrudging compliance. They can end up doing the behavior to avoid a penalty and never get to learn the beauty of heartfelt obedience.

Eventually, a rule for a rule's sake can create a rebellion similar to what Israel experienced towards the Law. Israel rebelled because they largely didn't trust the Person of God. They were only afraid of the authority of God. They most often didn't live out of relationship, but only an external, begrudging compliance to the Law. In this state, they couldn't obey from the heart. The Law was actually employed by God so their unrighteousness would be revealed, their sin would increase, and they would be compelled to cry out for the Messiah.

So, like Israel with God, our children, if they don't learn to trust us, may learn only to be afraid of our authority.

A guideline is much different. A guideline is worthless to a one-year-old but wonderfully life-giving to a ten-year-old. It gives more direction than directive. It employs a principle, a way of seeing, to help children understand how to navigate a variety of life decisions. The guideline is relationally communicated, allowing children to own their choices in heartfelt obedience rather than compliance to a rule. It communicates consequences and the basis, protection, and freedom within the truth being given. A guideline teaches excellent skills for navigating new choices ahead, choices that rules can never anticipate.

In brief, a rule says, "You will not do this or else." A guideline says, "Here is why you would choose these behaviors and not those. And I'll stand with you as you mature in these choices."

Let's look at an example of how we might start with rules and gradually move into guidelines at various ages.

Imagine standing with your child, looking out at the lightly traveled neighborhood street in front of your house.

15

When your child is two, the rule is clear and direct, without conditions or exceptions: "Do not go into the street." End of conversation. You, of course, surround the rule with your commitment, love, and consistency. But the rule is inflexible and there are age-appropriate consequences, explained and consistently enforced, for violating it. Because you love your children, you give the rule sometimes long before they are able to understand your reasons for giving it.

When your child is five, that same rule starts to be nuanced with further explanation, reasoning and consequences. "Don't go into the street without looking both ways for cars. Do you understand how important it is to look both ways? Sometimes there are cars coming that you won't be able to see right away. We want you to be safe because we love you so much. But if you ignore what I'm asking, you won't be able to cross the street to see your friends."

When your child is nine, you might find yourself with a football in your hand, asking your child, "You think we'd be okay to play catch in the street? What should we be concerned about?" You are now standing with your child, together exploring the risks, freedoms and consequences of an event. This conversation will now also inform future, yet-unseen opportunities and dangers. The rule has now morphed beatifully into a life-giving guideline.

Pretty cool stuff! Parents and kids learning how to navigate life together. Maybe your nine-year-old child in the street would smile and respond to you, "Dad, I've seen your passes. I'm not sure we're safe on any street."

Now, let's look at how we can help our children develop convictions. For convictions help form guidelines.

Consider a daughter's developing understanding of modesty.

At age sixteen it might not be good to start explaining modesty with these words; "You will not be leaving this house with that outfit on!" (Not that almost every parent of an adolescent hasn't said those words at one time or another.)

Remember, a guideline says, "Here is why you would choose these behaviors and not those. And I will stand with you as you mature into these choices."

A conviction is a particular belief or position that has become your own.

An age-related progression of conversations, modeling, and guidance helps nurture convictions. So maybe early on a mom begins a running conversation with her daughter as they walk through their daily lives, presenting from many angles how to begin to make choices consistent with who she wants to be.

Maybe at around age eight or nine you present this question: "How do I want to present myself to the world?" Your daughter may not have considered this before. But even at nine she can begin to understand how choices in the way she dresses and presents herself reflect her femininity, her identity, her person.

Somewhere around ten, you might help draw her into an awareness of the consequences of other girls' choices, in her own world and in the media surrounding her.

Again, all of this is in the context of seeing life together. It presupposes ongoing conversations, where such questions are not jarring or out of the blue.

Maybe by twelve, you begin to process together what choices of modesty or immodesty might affect boys.

There is no exact month when any discussion is best to begin. But there is an intentionality in watching for readiness to reason out the motives and values for their behaviors. There are many clumsy moments on this trail, more missteps than great moments of insight. There are more blank stares than "Oh, yes, my parent, I am beginning to see how this would change my life for the better. May I now serve you by setting the table and sorting out the recycling bin?"

Perhaps you get the point.

Everything about a guideline is more involved, more nuanced, and messier. Everything about a rule is simpler, clearer, cleaner, and more enforceable. But rules, unfortunately, don't create lasting, heartfelt obedience much after the age of nine.

If we don't understand these distinctions, we'll continue on the rule-making trajectory because it gives us the illusion of control. But, as the Clawsons heard in the podcast, the payoff is invariably this: rules will create either rebellious or compliant children.

Rules ultimately do not allow me to live out of the motivation of love. Only a motivation of love can free me to heartfelt obedience with sufficient and sustaining life motivation. A motivation that gets to trust the direction of Jesus instead of being compelled to comply with the "commands" of Jesus.

Compliance, though not an ideal state, can keep the yelling down for a while. And a home with less yelling gives everyone a chance to breathe and not be at each other's throats. But maybe we start to realize things are growing more distant and rigid. We admit it, if only to ourselves.

But now we're so tired.

We've been working so hard just making a living, securing their future, and figuring out how to afford the next vacation. A home of disrespectful preteenagers fighting with parents and each other was not an option. So, maybe we brought in a system that promised peace, order, and control. A consistent, well-structured system of clear and inviolable rules.

But maybe no one told us this way of running a home has a short shelf life. Or that our entire family would eventually resent it. And maybe by the time we discover it, it seems too late to go back and find our playfulness and closeness. Our kids have learned to find their own friends, their world, their place where they can feel more themselves. We still have meals together, still wake up in the same house, still all go to their sporting events. But the distance is there.

Learning to offer guidelines means we have to learn to think through life in terms of guidelines. It involves asking God to teach us the relational reasons behind our own choices. Many of us grew up in a house of rules, long after they were effective. We may have complied or rebelled and then just sort of settled into a vague semi-adherence to authority. We learned to parrot right answers. We learned to appear different than we actually were. We learned to turn off our hearts to some degree and look right more than being real. And it hasn't worked very well. We feel compromised in our own lives. We can't even live in the very system we are trying to promote to our kids! This can keep us feeling vaguely guilty most of the time. And unfit to parent out of our character and integrity.

A MATTER OF TRUST

By the time the four Clawsons meet up, it is nearly dark. Jim walked out onto the beach with his phone's flashlight to help them all find their way back to the condo. He thinks about things like that.

Later that evening, they walk three blocks down the boardwalk for pizza. Regardless of how they're doing, the Clawsons can always rally around pizza. On vacation, everyone gets to choose their own toppings, no matter how many pizzas it takes. Tonight, nothing has been forgiven or figured out. But issues have at least been suspended for several hours. Even Aiden is laughing on the walk back from the restaurant. Just moments ago from his balcony, a neighbor yelled down at Jim to stop singing so badly and loudly. "Hey you, buddy. Yeah, you, down there. I paid too much for this rental to listen to your off-key moaning." The man was only partly joking. Jim does sing badly. *Really* badly. But it has not deterred him from singing loudly. Madison could not be more embarrassed. But Aiden loves it. Watching his dad let loose a little in public makes the world feel more right.

Aiden and Madison are now in their own rooms. Jim and Sarah are downstairs in the living room, each pretending to read. Neither of them is ready to be lying in a bed next to each other. Pizza did not fix what is strained between them.

Jim and Sarah love each other. And for much of their marriage, they have enjoyed each other. This is not that particular time. It has been exceptionally tense and hard in this season of child-raising. Each of them believes the other is doing parenting mostly wrong. But they don't know how to talk about it. Their resentments are well defined. And intimacy is paying the price for it. They are learning to tiptoe around each other, rarely addressing the issues. They have believed that, if the kids don't know their parents fight, they will grow up healthier.

But every now and then it all boils up to the surface. Like on vacations. Where privacy is protected only by paper-thin walls.

Jim is generally louder and more opinionated. But in a battle of wills, Sarah can generally hold out much longer.

When he can no longer endure the very loud silence, Jim says, "So, lots of stuff to think about there. You know, in that podcast."

Without looking up from her book, Sarah says, "Yep."

More loud silence.

"Steinbeck wrote a bunch of books before anything really started selling for him. Did you know that?"

"Uh huh." Sarah is still pretending to read.

"I thought maybe he was famous from the start. But I see now he wasn't."

He answers himself, pretending they are having a conversation. "Yes, Jim, that's a fascinating observation."

His sarcasm is not wasted on her. If they weren't sprinting towards a conflict, they are now.

More minutes of pretend reading elapse.

Then, without looking up from her book Sarah says, "You know, you're going to lose her."

"What?"

Sarah is now looking at Jim. "She was just going over to Jeff's house. She knew what she needed to get done before we left. She and I had already talked about it. You treat her like a child."

"I'm sensing we're no longer discussing Steinbeck."

"I'm so pissed off at you, Jim!"

Jim stands and looks upstairs. "Can we not be so loud? We don't have to bring the kids in on this."

Sarah says, even more loudly, "Classic, Jim! Sure, let's maintain the freakin' illusion of a world for them where people never raise their voices, especially parents. Yes, Jim, let's all be nice and quiet. But you are going to lose us all if you keep powering up on them."

Jim whispers loudly, "I'm not powering up! Maybe I'm just the only one interested in good parenting."

"You're right, Jim. If humiliating your daughter in public is good parenting, then yes, perhaps you *are* the only one."

"For God's sake, Sarah, stop it! We're on vacation. Why do we have to do this every time? You wait to drag me into our biggest fights on vacation. Can't we just have a good time with our kids?"

"You do something so overpoweringly stupidly insensitive and then we're all supposed to be happy and move on, like nothing happened? You think you won, don't you? You didn't, Jim. You're going to lose them, both of them."

She shuts the book more loudly than necessary for it to close. And then come words that reveal the depth of her disappointment in their marriage. Words she has thought but never before said to Jim.

"And if you didn't notice, you're losing me. I don't want to talk to you. I'm going to bed."

Jim is determined to have the last word.

"That works well then because I don't want to talk to you either."

She storms into the bedroom, closing the door more loudly than necessary for it to latch.

Jim sighs to himself, as he steps outside and over the waist high patio wall. "Damn!"

The next day the Clawsons all take their time getting down to the beach. They cover their familiar summer beach spot with blankets, towels, ice chests, and umbrellas.

Neither Jim nor Sarah brings up the previous night's talk. Apparently, with their windows open to the sound of the waves, the kids didn't hear their parents arguing. Over the years, Jim and Sarah have learned to compartmentalize their fights, continuing the next day like nothing happened. It doesn't work in the long run. But it's what their parents did. It never worked for them either.

After lunch, Madison suddenly gets up from her blanket, brushes sand off, and begins walking toward the north pier. She's wearing a swimsuit top and cut-off shorts. Her hands are buried deep into the pockets. Staring out at the water, her face carries the expression of someone small carrying something that's too big.

Jim notices but waits a few moments before he follows her, not wanting to be conspicuous. But he waits too long and loses her in the crush of humanity around the entrance to the pier. He gambles that she has walked onto the pier. It is one of her favorite places. He eventually spots her, standing down at the far end, woven in among families of half a dozen ethnicities fishing. The group is a blur of laughter, noise and motion, wildly pulling flopping mackerel onto the rough wooden planks. For thirty yards of pier, it's utter chaos and delight.

Madison stands motionless in a crowd on fast forward. She stares at the ocean. Jim watches his daughter for quite a while. Time slows down in front of him.

He recalls the afternoon he first taught his beautiful little girl to cast and unhook a fish on this very pier. How she squeamishly turned away as he put a small fish on the line for bait. And then the wild pandemonium when a mackerel strike bent her fishing pole down hard. She squealed, jumping up and down. "Dad, we got one! Dad, is it a big one? Dad, let me get it!" She wouldn't let him take the fish off. She wanted to learn how to do it herself. And she did! She used pliers to pull out the hook and then tossed the bloody fish into the nearby water bucket.

Jim breaks into an involuntarily wide smile as he recalls those nearby applauding and walking over to pat his daughter on her ball cap.

Life snaps back to full speed as Jim is jolted to the scene in the front yard from a couple nights ago. Everything was so simple when she was little. Now it's all so strained and complex, and he doesn't know what to do.

Phrases from the parenting podcast play over and over.

"The degree to which your children trust you is the degree to which they will let you love them and influence them."

She doesn't trust me right now. I'm not sure I trust me. I think she used to trust me. Or at least like me.

When Madison was three or four she would block the door as he was preparing to leave for work. Her little pigtails would bounce as she'd stomp and yell, "Don't go, Daddy!"

I used to be what that song says: "the god and the weight of her world."

Jim misses the girl he used to make up songs with. He misses camping out with her in the backyard and lying on their trampoline, looking up into the night, wondering out loud how far the sky goes. But the heart of that girl is now three oceans away.

He is unwittingly pacing a fifteen-yard stretch of the pier, back and forth.

I don't know how to do this. She gets angry at something. Then she gets disrespectful. Then I get angry. Then my anger becomes everyone's issue. I hate it.

What did that woman say? If I don't let them tell me how I'm affecting them, then it will come out in anger. Then I'll end up reacting to their anger instead of hearing what they're trying to tell me.

Jim mumbles to himself, "It's like they have cameras in our home."

He weaves his way through the fishing frenzy, toward Madison. She's either indifferent to his presence or so deep in thought that she doesn't notice him. Jim is now standing next to her, resting his elbows on the pier railing. He looks out at the ocean alongside her.

"Can we talk?"

No response. Just mackerel flopping and churning in water-filled buckets behind them.

"Madison, I'd like to ask you how I'm affecting you."

She shakes her head. "Don't even."

"Don't even what?"

"You don't even have the line right."

"What line?"

"The line from your podcast." She adjusts her sunglasses at the bridge of her nose.

"You were listening?"

"Yeah, well."

"But you had your ear buds in."

"I do it all the time."

"Do what?"

"Wear the ear buds without the sound on. It's the only way we get to hear what you people are actually thinking."

"Huh." Jim says under his breath. "Sort of like players stealing signs from the catcher."

"What?"

"Nothing."

"Dad, I already told you. And you didn't listen. I'd tell you some more, but what's the point?"

"Well, that wasn't exactly what I—"

"You don't listen to me."

Madison turns around and begins walking back towards the beach, vaguely nodding for him to follow, signaling their conversation is over.

"Ear buds in without the sound on," Jim mumbles. "Brilliant."

Madison nearly smiles. Something in his attempt at vulnerability allows Madison to let her dad catch up. They don't talk for the entire walk back down the beach. But Jim is being let back in to Madison's world. At least a little. His daughter is walking down the beach with him. Maybe a step or two ahead of him. But they're walking. And for now, that is enough.

INSIDE THE EPISODE

On that pier with Madison, Jim was trying out a profound life truth. He was doing it poorly. But still, his willingness to risk movement toward Madison by starting to own his wrong carries a significance he cannot yet understand.

As a parent, there is nothing more important than earning your children's trust.

Nothing.

The degree to which your children trust you is the degree to which they will let you love them. No matter how much love you have to give them.

We may have great intentions to pass on values, beliefs, wisdom, and truths. We may faithfully love, protect, and direct our children. But if they don't trust us, nothing is really happening.

Consider the earlier statement about God: "Because God's primary goal is earning my trust so He can love me and increasingly mature me, correct my behavior, and free my life, I will attempt to offer the same for my child." And when my child trusts me, I can give love that can be received, I can teach truth, and I can provide guidance. It's the exact same pattern to health for me and my child as it is with God and me!

Don't forget—the heart is accessed only by trust.

We know what we struggled with. And we don't want our children to have to go through the same. So without even asking if it works, we presume that controlling our kids with stern authority, shame, or an appeal to disappointed conditional acceptance will protect them. It is painful to discover that just knowing we want to protect is not the same as the ability to protect them.

None of us want to be our children's truant officers. None of us want to win by power, loudness, or taking away privileges. But it's possible to wake up one day and discover this is the role we've taken on. Techniques, formulas, and strategies coming from a faulty application of spiritual principles appear to ensure success. We can be easily seduced into imagining that, if we can just get our kids to behave, our job is mostly done. But if this is how you think about parenting, like Jim, you may find yourself having a hard conversation with your children. A conversation about how you are not trusted to influence their hearts. And it will break your heart.

If you are a new parent, you don't have to take this road. Even if you are a parent of a teenager six months from moving out, it's not too late to reverse that path and the damage done. God has created incredible hope in the family.

It's never too late to find and reoffer that hope. It is never too late.

25

EPISODE
FOUR

YESTERDAY IS GONE

None of the Clawsons are late sleepers. Even on vacation. By 7:45 a.m. they're already up and ready to head down Highway 1.

Before heading up the coast, they plan to spend some time with Sarah's parents, sixty miles south in Encinitas.

As they planned the vacation, they had already talked about this. But Jim asks again, "Do we really have to visit your parents on this trip? It's kind of out of the way."

"They're my parents!" Sarah reacts, with no small measure of hurt. "You can't just wipe them from the record. We're going to see *your* parents. Right?"

"Yeah, but my parents are on the way."

"We could have come up through San Diego. Then they would have been on the way."

Jim bluffs, avoiding logic. "Well, we could have come up through the Dominican Republic, and a whole lot of people would have been on the way."

Aiden calls from the back seat, "What does that even mean?"

Madison breaks in. "About the AC vents. Anything at all for us back here?"

Jim could happily avoid Sarah's parents on vacations—and nearly every other occasion. And her parents would not be entirely unhappy if they could see the family without Jim.

Here's a direct quote from Sarah's dad, Hal:

"He couldn't have been a doctor? What's a *healthcare supervisor* anyway? Who studies to become a healthcare supervisor? Does he get paid by the hour? Maybe it's just me, but I don't get it. You know, we told her all along, 'You could have married Kevin Reynolds. He's got his own practice.' We must have told her that a hundred times. Didn't we? What's not to like about Dr. Kevin Reynolds? But no, she's got to marry a healthcare supervisor."

Madison and Aiden don't mind visiting Sarah's parents if only because they have a giant-screen television. *A 72-inch screen.* The Clawsons own a 42-inch screen. This comparison has been noted several times already on the trip. Jim is almost certain that Hal bought the television just to show the grandkids he's a better provider than their dad.

Sarah loves her parents. But visiting them is never easy. She sees way too much of herself in them. Especially her mom. Leslie has a way of tucking a jab, a critique, or a moral lesson into almost every conversation. Nagging moralism wrapped in religious justification is a hard pill for anyone to swallow. And Leslie has religious nagging down to an art form. Sarah always feels like her mom is never quite satisfied with her.

The last time Hal and Leslie came to Phoenix for the holidays, they stayed in the Clawsons' spare bedroom.

Big mistake.

"Sarah, honey, do you just let the kids decide when they go to bed? Isn't that something you want to be in charge of? You need to put a schedule on the refrigerator with clear and specific rules. That's what I did. Remember? That way everyone knows what's expected of them. You'd sure have less of a fight than you do with Madison, come bedtime."

Leslie has a PhD in everyone else's business. You can't tell Leslie *anything*. Leslie can't be told. Just ask Hal.

The visit went from horrible to horribler when Madison was

making fun of Leslie behind her back. While Leslie went on about the refrigerator schedule, Madison was in the next room animatedly acting out Leslie's words to her little brother, who had just been minding his own business. Aiden remembers the incident well. He got in a lot of trouble for "disrespect" because he's the one who laughed out loud. When everyone entered the room, Madison shrugged her shoulders as if to say, "Wish I knew what he was laughing at."

But now they're in Encinitas, two days into the visit. Sarah feels like she's been holding her breath, walking through a minefield the entire time. For the most part, the stay has been without incident. But the tension could drive a non-smoker like Sarah to light up an entire pack of nonfiltered cigarettes.

Later in the evening, after her parents go to bed, Sarah puts on a sweatshirt and slips out onto the beach, a block from her parents' home.

Like Jim, she can't shake some phrases from the podcast:

"If I adopt a sin-management theology, those who follow me are led into the same unhealthy pattern."

Sarah is carrying her sandals and walking ankle deep in the ocean along the Encinitas shoreline. And again, she is thinking out loud, but to whom? Herself? God?

"It's happened to me. I've followed my mom into the same ridiculous patterns. They didn't work for her, and they're definitely not working for me."

Sarah is realizing she goads her kids into submission. Maybe not Madison, as much as she has tried. But definitely Aiden. Just like her mother, she has chipped away at him with incessant commentary.

"Throwing edicts at us was her way of making sure we showed well in public, without her having to get in the trenches and get dirty with our emotions and drama. There was probably a moment when she realized it wasn't working. When she realized we weren't enjoying each other. But Mom must have stuffed it away, rationalizing that she was 'not supposed to be her children's friend, but their parent!' That her kids would not grow up like 'those Slocum kids,' prowling the neighborhood well after the streetlights came on. Even if her kids were miserable, they would thank her for it when they grew up. Well, I'm an adult now. And I am not thankful. I resent her manipulative clichés now as much I did then.

"Do Madison and Aiden make fun of me behind my back? Did they try for a while and then get tired of pretending they could keep up with the continual droning of my demand?

"Jim was right. We should have never come down here. It's never good."

Sarah has been rehearsing these thoughts for nearly three miles. She suddenly realizes how far she is from her parents' house. The adrenaline wave of her angst has receded. She's now concerned she might not be able to make it back. It's too late to be alone on this dark and lonely stretch of beach.

Sarah pulls out her phone and calls Jim. She asks him to meet her at a coffee shop she can see from the beach.

Ten minutes later they're sitting across from each other at Surf Dog's Java Hut. The place has been closed for hours but there's a picnic table outside. The moon is out and a streetlight from Highway 101 shines near them, so they're able to see each other.

"You were right, Jim. We shouldn't have come down here. How's my dad treating you?"

"Get this. He asked if we make the kids get vaccinations. Vaccinations! I didn't know what to say. I answered, 'Maybe.' Who answers 'maybe'? It's a yes or no question! But your dad is like kryptonite to me. I lose the ability to think. I can't believe I said 'maybe.' Your dad got up, mumbled something about healthcare and 'those money-printing socialists,' and stormed off to the kitchen."

"He likes you, Jim. You just happen to be his daughter's husband. Kind of like Jeff. A nice kid, who happens to have met your daughter."

"You've had better analogies."

Sarah senses Jim's frustrated exhaustion, so she changes gears to what she has been waiting to ask. "I need you to tell me—am I like my mom? Do I make everyone feel judged all the time?"

"I can't see your eyes out here in the dark. Is this a trick question?"

"I need you to tell me."

There is an awkward pause.

"This reminds me of that commercial where Abe Lincoln's wife asks him, 'Does this dress make me look heavy?'"

"So, you're saying I'm heavy?"

"Perhaps you're missing the subtle point of this analogy."

"So, you're saying I *am* like my mom."

Jim takes a deep breath.

"How about how you're *not* like her? She would never ask anyone the question you just asked me. She'd never want to know. She would never ever let anyone tell her the truth about herself. So, no, in that way, you are not like her."

"Jim, being here with my parents, I see that so much of the way I parent has come from them. I feel totally unequipped to parent our kids. But I make them feel like it's their fault. And I feel you're too much for them, so I try and protect them from you. But I'm realizing someone needs to protect them from me."

Sarah turns away, as though she's finding these insights in the asphalt four feet from their table. Jim stares at her and smiles. He's so attracted to her right now, under the street light in this vulnerable, honest moment. "Sarah, the chances of me screwing up this moment are astronomical. Could we just go back?"

"I know how this plays out. I will go to bed and when I wake up I will go on like nothing happened. It's how I survive."

Jim calmly answers her, "Then let's not. Let's not go on like nothing happened. Sarah, I don't know how you'll hear this, but I feel closer to you in these few moments than I have in months."

Silence.

Jim stands up and nods toward the car. Sarah stands and says, "You didn't screw up this moment." She pauses. "You didn't fully answer the question about Abe Lincoln. But I think I'm going to let you off the hook. Yes, let's get back. Did anyone ask where I was?"

"Your mom did. I quote: 'Jim, have you seen Sarah? I just need to ask her which service you all want to go to in the morning.'"

"Service? Why is she saying that? We're on vacation. She knows we're not going to church."

"Don't shoot me. I'm just the messenger."

"Their pastor gives me a headache. He ends half of his sentences with, 'Am I right?' No, we are not going to that church!"

31

"Talk to your mom. I'm not getting in the middle of this. I've got my own battles going on. I had to tell your dad, 'No, I'd rather you not have the kids watch Ultimate Fighting Championship matches with you.' I still don't know if he was being serious. I'm telling you, the man gets in my head!"

Sarah laughs.

"I'm sorry. It's complicated. Dad's this 'in charge,' high-voltage businessman. But as long as I can remember, when it comes to parenting, it's all Mom. Dad isn't passive-aggressive. He's just passive. He's let Mom do it all. I think he's afraid to cross her or get involved, for fear if he did he'd have to do some actual parenting. He always overspent on us kids, especially at birthdays and holidays. I think it was his way of proving he loved us too. It's the one place where he was willing to risk the verbal beating from Mom."

"Yeah, well, I wouldn't mind his unhealthy compensating extending to his son-in-law."

Sarah, still stuck on the thing about church, says, "We need to leave early in the morning if we're going to get up to Monterey by evening. We are not going to their church."

As they both walk to the car, Jim mutters, "I said 'maybe' to your dad. It was a yes or no question."

By 8 a.m. the next morning they're back in the car. Jim sits in the driver's seat with the door open, calculating the 415 miles of mostly winding highway from Encinitas to Monterey. Sarah and the kids are lugging the last of their luggage into the back of the car. Sarah had made it quite clear to her parents last night that they would not be attending church with them. But "quite clear" doesn't mean that went over well. As Leslie and Hal start to leave the house for church, Leslie meets them at the car, hugging each of the kids.

Then, true to form, she leaves Sarah with a predictable admonition. "I still think I'd want to show an example for the kids that God doesn't take vacations. But don't mind me. We're certainly not their parents."

Jim grips the steering wheel like he's attempting to choke the life out of a rabid wolverine. He breathes in a long audible breath.

"Our church service is broadcast on the local radio station," Leslie continues. "Maybe you could listen in the car."

Sarah's parents pull out of the driveway. Jim starts the car, adjusts

32

the rearview mirror, and peers at both Madison and Aiden in the backseat. Both of them are eye-rolling in acknowledgment of their grandmother's jab. Jim shifts into reverse and backs out the driveway, waving at Hal and Leslie, grinning an overdone smile, "Kids, what Grandma said, let it be a lesson for all of us."

"What lesson?" Aiden asks.

"Son, I have absolutely no idea."

The route ahead is winding, and Jim suddenly recalls their drive through Wolf Creek Pass in Colorado last summer. Things didn't go so well for Aiden in the backseat. Jim jumps out at the first convenience store he sees to pick up some Dramamine.

Fool me twice, he thinks to himself. *Not today, universe.*

Somewhere past Thousand Oaks, they hit a construction back-up. Twenty minutes drag from one exit sign to the next. The illusion of movement and private space evaporates as they inch along.

Madison pretends she's choking in the back seat. "AC… Can't. Get…AC." Then, to the surprise of everyone, she says, "It's fine if you want to play that podcast."

Behind her façade of disinterest, Madison is deeply hooked on what this lady is saying.

Madison knows something is wrong—with her family, with life. She doesn't quite yet know why she feels the way she does. She just knows her heart hurts. She is becoming cynical and withdrawn from them. She is usually looking for a fight, even if she doesn't care about the issue at all. She's losing hope. Hope that her parents will know the real Madison. Hope they will be able to handle the real truth about her. Hope that they'll ever know the things she's stopped telling them. And she is losing hope that the faith her parents have raised her to believe is capable of correcting the hypocrisy she sees around her.

Maybe it's the kindness of the woman's voice. Maybe it's that what she's teaching sounds so different from what Madison has heard in her home. She's having a hard time understanding why they would keep letting this play. Regardless, Madison has become a cheerleader for this podcast on parenting.

Sarah cues up her phone and starts the podcast.

"So far, we've been walking through foundational truths largely available to everyone. But today we are expressing the power and basis behind these truths available to parents who are believers in Christ.

"To engage a new life demands you believe in a grace that not only gets you to heaven, but one that has already changed you completely and is maturing you now.

"Grace that appeals to your new nature of Christ fused in you. Grace that appeals to an already accomplished righteousness in you. Grace that appeals to an already accomplished holiness in you. Grace that convinces you that you are no longer who you were.

"Do you know you are completely righteous and holy, right now, completely? Not just some day, after enough strenuous diligence and endless performance. But right now?

"You. Right now.

"Righteous. Holy.

"Nothing you believe and depend upon is more magnificently freeing than this single truth: You are no longer who you were, even on your worst day. Trusting and leaning upon 'Christ in you' is the source of every shred of strength, joy, healing, and peace.

"For you and for your child."

Madison calls out from the back seat. "Pause, please."
Sarah turns it off.
Madison asks, "Do we believe this stuff?"
Still looking forward, Sarah responds, "What do you mean, Madison?"
"I mean, we never talk this way. Ever."
Jim doesn't say anything, but he knows Madison is telling the truth.
By now the traffic opens up and the Subaru is back up to speed. Getting out of the traffic feels like a natural transition from the

awkwardness of the moment. Everyone goes back to what they were doing earlier.

Everyone but Madison, who now has this new thought playing in her head: *"You are no longer who you were."*

The Clawsons wind their way up through Malibu and Santa Barbara. The morning's marine layer is breaking up and it is turning out to be a majestic California coast day.

Aiden encourages the family to get out into the sunshine with these words: "Dad, I'm gonna throw up."

Unfortunately, they're still four miles from Morro Bay. So Jim envisions himself as Captain Kirk at the helm of the starship Enterprise and pushes the Subaru into warp drive. Sooner than even he imagined, Jim is taking the exit ramp leading to a beach none of them have ever seen before. Aiden barrels out of the car and heads for a nearby clump of trees. The anticipated outcome didn't come out, so to speak. False alarm, but still alarming. Jim, Sarah, and Madison each grab blankets, chairs, the cooler, and arms full of grocery bags. They give Aiden a pass on this lug-everything trip down to the beach.

Morro Bay is the unofficial transition point between Southern and Northern California beaches. Cypress trees line their path, bending away from the ocean. Soon they are standing on sand with more driftwood than they've ever seen. Morro Rock, an immense volcanic landmark, looms in front of them, fifty yards from shore. Southern California beaches are largely devoid of interesting shells, beach glass, and driftwood. But this stretch is raw and windy, unpredictable, almost dangerous. It all feels uncharted and alive. This beach, in a way, is reflecting life in this family.

For the first ten years, parenting sort of felt like a Southern California beach. Fun, simple, predictable, expensive, crowded. Side by side with other vacationing families, dragging boogie boards onto a raked section of sand in front of a resort hotel. Parenting felt more domesticated, controllable. Today parenting feels like the beach at Morro Bay. Uneven sand. The beach covered with kelp and ocean grass, and no resort employee to rake it away.

Neither Aiden nor Madison have been to this stretch of California before. On this less-tamed beach, their parents seem more fun, hip, and wise than they did half an hour before.

Aiden calls out, as he runs in front of the rest, "This is awesome!" He throws a piece of driftwood at the water. "Why haven't you brought us here before?"

This strand of Morro Bay beach is about three miles long. During the next several hours, each of them scatters aimlessly over much of it—exploring tide pools and looking for beach glass, shells, and interesting driftwood. They eventually meet back up on spread-out blankets to make sandwiches and stare out at the sea.

"Potato chips in your sandwich, Aiden? Why?" Madison makes a face like she's accusing him of pouring mustard on cereal.

"Because it's great."

"No. Just no! The chips sit next to the sandwich on a plate. We have rules as a society. It's what separates us from the animals."

Aiden wads even more chips into his sandwich, takes a giant bite and then opens his mouth wide at Madison to show her what food looks like, all mixed together.

"Oh, my gosh. I think I'm gonna be sick."

Jim looks over at Madison, smiles, and briefly opens his mouth, filled with a variety of chewed up picnic mush.

"That's sick. Mom, do something."

"They're just having fun, Madison."

"Men are animals. Gross, stupid animals."

Jim and Aiden then look at each other and try to bark. Which makes them laugh so hard, they spit out some of their food. More barking. And more laughter. Like they are the two funniest people on earth.

This quality of interaction dominates the next few minutes.

A family, unrehearsed, unplugged, on vacation.

No one is in a hurry to get back to the car.

But the thin clouds have deceived them. The sun is doing much damage. By the time they return to the car, they are all sunburned. None of them feel pain yet. But they most certainly will.

It's not that they don't have sunscreen. Madison takes it from the cup holder in the back seat as they climb back into their Subaru. "Sunscreen spray, anyone?"

As they back out of the parking lot, Aiden yells, "Wait!" He has just realized his hat is on a rock back near the shore. "Stop. My hat! My hat!" He's out of the car by now. He motions to where they were, half a mile ago. "It's back there!"

Jim is irritated. He has their hotel arrival time down to the minute. And now irresponsibility is messing up his metrics.

And any other time Jim might say, "Get back in the car, Aiden. It's a stupid, ten-dollar hat. We'll get another one." Or, "You kids have just got to learn to look around before you leave a place. With everything we've lost, we could take a vacation to Hawaii."

But he doesn't do that this time.

This time a spiritual reality is swirling around in the moment: *Truth only transforms when it is trusted.*

He is still irritated. But Jim is deciding to trust something he's heard on the podcasts. Believed words are now merging with his heart and coming out in an action so qualitatively different it surprises even him.

He turns back to Aiden, smiles and says, "It's okay, bud. Let's all go back and get your hat."

That was it.

No embarrassing lecture, no rolling of the eyes, no disgusted glance to his wife, no shaking of his head, no sigh, no "Hurry up and go get it then. We're already late!"

The four of them walk back down to the beach to retrieve Aiden's hat.

Jim is not even sure what's going on. He just knows it's different.

None of this is wasted on Madison.

She walks behind the others on the way back. She is wondering about what she has just seen. Was this real? Or just a blip on the screen, that'll last only until Aiden's water glass is spilled at dinner?

"You are no longer who you were."

INSIDE THE EPISODE

What we believe happened in that first moment of trusting Jesus affects everything after. That start is called "justification." A five-dollar word, but it's a good one—it means to be made right. Not just the ability to one day become more right. But to have been made right already! Not sinless. And not as healthy or mature as we will one day become. But in a completely right condition. Right now.

Not by our own doing, but by Christ's doing it in us, at that first moment of trusting Him.

Some believe that, through sincere diligence, they will change into someone better. They will become more right. Their confidence to change centers on their focused self-effort.

But the very essence of who we now are is completely changed at the moment we put our faith in Him. We have absolute fused union with the God of the universe!

What happens when you mix lemonade with iced tea? You don't get part iced tea and part lemonade. You get an Arnold Palmer, right? You don't get iced tea on the bottom and lemonade on the top. You don't get part Arnold and part Palmer. You get a beverage that is molecularly and newly woven together.

That's us with Jesus. Not Jesus up there, or over there. Not Jesus some of the time indwelling us. Not part of Jesus. But all of Jesus integrated, amalgamated, merged with all of us! A completely new creature.

Christ in us.

Incapable of identifying where one starts and the other ends. Incapable of sorting out the human and God sections. Intermeshed entirely. That's how indelibly God has inhabited you!

So, our confidence to mature is placed squarely in trust of our new identity in Jesus! This does not mean we don't fail. Like a lanky junior high kid who doesn't know what to do with a growth spurt, we are, for quite some time, clumsy and odd feeling in this new reality. We will fail. Often. But in the end we get to trust who God has made us. And it will actually eventually start to wonderfully change our behaviors. We will love more and sin less. That deserves a repeat: We will love more and sin less. Because we are depending upon this "Christ in us" reality.

This means I never define myself any longer as a "loser" or a "failure." I no longer get to give myself permission to fail because, "Well, that's how it's always been. I always mess it up eventually."

Living out of your new identity may change what you read and which preachers you listen to. You may become more discerning and careful to see which methodology they are emphasizing and their motive behind it. You can begin to listen for it in your own thinking and verbal approach to parenting your own kids.

Yes, of course, we mature in that righteousness. We continually discover more how to live in that righteousness. But it's all there in us, right now! All of it.

Do you know what would change if you and I believed that?

Ab-so-lute-ly ev-er-y-thing!

In many believing homes, parents are convinced we are all only saved sinners (heavy emphasis on sinner). So, while behaviors may appear good, no one's heart is really to be trusted. This "saved sinner" theology carries this cynical and erroneous presumption: At their core, our kids mostly want to be bad.

Left alone long enough, without enough control, rules, and shame, our children would ditch their Sunday school class, get into a car with a carnival operator, and drive to an abandoned warehouse to empty a two-liter bottle of a beverage named Old Mr. Boston. Purchased with a fake ID.

Such wonky theology says Jesus only saved us. We get to go to heaven, but nothing in us really changed. Our kids will change only through constant lecturing, control, and reminding them to not ever trust themselves. Obviously this affects how we parent. And it affects how our kids respond to our parenting.

Some of us are parenting children who do not yet know Jesus. We can parent now in the hope of them becoming believers. Anyone created in the image of God responds best when they are treated with genuine love and respect. God's image in every child calls out for these two hallmarks of dignity: love and respect. When parents respect their children, and siblings respect each other, no matter how young they are, a family nurtures the beginning foundations of trust and health.

Ah, but for those parenting children who have trusted Jesus, these next verses are true for them, regardless of their maturity, always!

"I have been crucified with Christ; and it is no longer I who live, but Christ lives in me; and the life which I now live in the flesh I live by faith in the Son of God, who loved me and gave Himself up for me."

Galatians 2:20

"Put on the new self, which in the likeness of God has been created in righteousness and holiness of the truth."

Ephesians 4:24

There is a world of difference in seeing your children as saved sinners or as young, maturing saints! Once you are vitally convinced of that, it allows you to appeal to a new place to effect behavioral change. It allows you to teach them who they really are.

At the core, your believing children want to do right!

And once they trust His new life in them as their resource, they will inevitably and invariably grow to love more and sin less.

Let that sink in for a minute. Or two.

BACK TO EPISODE 4: YESTERDAY IS GONE

The 17-Mile Drive from Carmel to Monterey is one of the most picturesque stretches along the Pacific coast. As the sun begins to sink behind a bank of clouds, the Clawsons are right in the middle of that drive.

No one in this car is fully appreciating the moment. It's been four hours since Morro Bay. With each bend of the ocean-hugging road, sunburn is exacting its toll.

When he was a boy, Jim's parents took the family to Monterey for vacation every summer. There are unforgettable memories here. Jim still has the portrait done by a beach artist at Monterey's Fisherman's Wharf that summer of 1986. Jim was eight. The family stayed right next to the wharf. His parents would allow him and his two older brothers to wander those two blocks by themselves. They spent entire mornings at the Monterey Bay Aquarium, staring at fish that seemed to be from another planet. Jim traces his present dread of eels to those days.

Then there was *Cannery Row*. Steinbeck would later become his favorite author and Cannery Row one of his favorite books.

When Jim and Sarah first started thinking about this vacation, they knew they would come here. And the Spindrift Inn would be their hotel. The Clawsons are not wealthy. But for these two nights, they have decided to pull out all the stops, shoot the moon. The Spindrift is built directly on the site where Jim's family used to stay. It is nicer than any hotel they have ever stepped into. With his travel points, he was even able to swing for two suites! If there are conflicts in the family, this hotel should calm them for a while.

But no hotel can trump bad sunburn. This first evening the Clawsons all retreat to bed early. Sarah purchases a bottle of aloe vera lotion in the lobby gift store. There is audible yelping and sticking to hotel sheets this first night.

But the following day is one where reality actually does exceed anticipation. For each of them. Aiden is allowed to play on the elevators, all by himself. Madison orders breakfast out on her balcony and is sending pictures to everyone she knows. Jim and Sarah open their patio sliding glass door and let the ocean breeze envelop the room. They do little more than sit around in bathrobes, leisurely reading the paper, working crosswords and drinking coffee poured from a silver carafe.

Late in the morning, they all meet up in the lobby to walk to the aquarium.

Once there, Jim can barely take in the huge wall-to-wall aquarium of radiantly colored fish. He is also completely enjoying his kids staring at them. Sarah is reading all the virtual tour pieces most people ignore. Madison is sitting close to her brother, both of them oohing and aahing each time the school moves in neon-florescent unison.

By six, they've started working their way down the street toward the wharf. After sampling Styrofoam cups of clam chowder at the entrances of several restaurants, they walk into the Old Fisherman's Grotto. It's one of the nicest and oldest restaurants on the pier. Jim's family used to eat here each time they came to Monterey.

While waiting for their meals, Sarah says, "All right, everyone, name your best meal on the trip so far."

Jim proudly proclaims it was the sandwich he made at Morro Bay. Jim likes the way he makes sandwiches. Sarah liked the pizza in Newport Beach. Madison argues that the cream puffs at the donut shop near her grandparents' house should be everyone's favorite.

Aiden responds, "Here."

Madison rolls her eyes. "What? We haven't even eaten yet! Aiden, you're so lame!"

And the moment she says it, she regrets it.

He is embarrassed, feeling like the stupid little brother. Again.

As Aiden has gone quieter in the last several years, the other three have sort of unconsciously gone on without him. At first, they just covered for him, trying to not make him feel embarrassed for being so quiet. They all naturally just kept telling stories, loudly arguing, and giving their opinions. All except Aiden. But now it has become normal. For everyone except Aiden. He just feels increasingly embarrassed, stupid, and small.

Aiden gets one word out: "Nevermind."

Sarah touches his arm. "Aiden, your sister was the lame one. So, why is this your favorite place?"

"I don't know."

"I'm sorry, Aiden. Mom's right. I'm the lame one. Why is this your favorite place?"

"Nothing."

"Come on, Aiden. Why?"

After a few seconds more, Aiden says, "Because we're all happy."

Everyone knows Aiden is right. This family has not been very happy lately. At least not at the same time. Not in a long time.

The podcast woman said earlier that the most critical relational development time in a child's life is age nine to ten.

Sarah thinks, *That's Aiden. Right in the middle of the most critical period of his life. And he's the one least spoken to or listened to.*

"Aiden," Sarah says, as she turns back to her son, "What makes it unhappy in our family?"

Each of them would like to know his answer.

"You and Dad don't have very much fun."

Jim can't believe what he's hearing. "You're right. Keep showing us how to have fun, Aiden. Even if it means you and I have to gross your sister out."

This makes everyone but Madison smile and gets the awkwardness off of Aiden.

"Okay, Dad. I'll try."

The rest of the family continues in conversation. Jim does not. He is rehearsing a statement from that first day of the podcast. Suddenly, it makes sense to him.

"Teach your children and they will learn something. Model for your children and they will experience something."

Jim blurts out, "Excuse me, everyone. I would like to say something."

First, Aiden's vulnerability. And now, Jim asking permission to speak. The Clawsons are well off the grid.

"I just wanted to tell you, Madison, that I'm sorry."

Suddenly their table is the quietest in the restaurant.

These are not words anyone is used to hearing Jim say. Especially not in front of all of them.

"The other night was not about you. It was about me. I'm not sure why I did that, yelling at you in front of the whole neighborhood. But I did it. And I'm very sorry. No, wait. That's not entirely true. I know why I did it. I'm afraid.

"I'm afraid I'm losing you. I'm afraid I'm going to lose you to some kid with a weird haircut that I don't trust. So I get all tough guy, because I've got to have something I can control because I feel like everything's out of control. Anyway, I think that's what I was doing in the yard. I embarrassed you. And I'm very sorry, Madison."

"When we as parents are honest about our own fears and feelings with our children, they will learn to be honest with themselves, and us as well."

He waits for a moment before saying, "Does that make any sense?" And then, "Do you believe me?"

There is suddenly no one else in the restaurant. Only the two of them and the question: "Do you believe me?"

Madison is undone. In a moment, she invisibly shifts from a posture of self-protection to pain. Pain from having to admit her dad has hurt her. Many times. She involuntarily wells up with tears.

"Madison, say something. Please."

Madison is young but discerning. She knows enough to understand how she answers is crucial. A confession like this might take another fourteen years.

She chooses her words carefully. "Dad, I want to."

"I'm not sure I always give you a reason to believe me." Jim wipes salt off the table, too uncomfortable to yet look directly at his daughter.

Then, he looks fully at her. "I want you to know I mean it. I'm just a freaked-out dad who doesn't know what to do with a fourteen-year-old daughter. I guess I'm just trying to say ... I just don't want to lose you."

Tears are now rolling down her face. She looks away, suddenly aware again of every other person in the room.

Like so many dads, Jim has been convinced that, if he were to own his failure in front of his family without covering it in rationalization or bravado, he would irreparably damage his respect and authority. In truth, families are actually hardwired to even more vitally trust, respect, and follow a father who is vulnerable and honest about his failures and limitations.

The server barges into the moment, asking if they're ready to order. And the moment evaporates.

But it will not be forgotten by anyone for a long time.

After dinner, the Clawsons walk back toward the hotel on the boardwalk. Jim and Aiden are a few feet ahead.

Sarah calls out, "Hey, Madison and I are going to stay back for a little bit. I've got a room key. We'll meet up with you two in a bit."

"Okay. Maybe Aiden and I will go walk the streets for a little while. I promised we'd look in some shops to see if we could find him a shirt with fish on it. I've got my phone on if you need anything."

Sarah and Madison purchase a small bag of sea-salt chocolates before sitting down on a bench overlooking the water. The chocolates now sit between them. The sky is turning purple as the two take off their sandals and put their feet up on the railing. They are overlooking bobbing boats and listening to the sound of the ropes securing them being stretched by the lapping water.

"When you were a girl, did you tell your mom stuff?"

"Stuff?"

"Yes. Like, hard stuff?"

Sarah feels a rush of blood to her face to brace for what could be coming.

"Fair question. What kind of hard stuff?"

"I don't know. Hard stuff. Stuff you might be afraid to tell anyone."

"No. I don't think my mom and I have ever really had that kind of relationship."

"I didn't think so."

Sarah taps her sandals against the bench to a song coming from a saxophone player down the pier, in a concerted effort to appear unfazed for whatever "hard stuff" Madison potentially might be about to reveal.

Sarah ventures, "Do we have that kind of relationship?"

Both are looking straight ahead, out into the harbor lights.

"I don't know …"

"So try me. Is there any specific hard stuff you're thinking about?"

"No."

Then Madison changes her mind.

"Yes. It's Jeff. Mom, he's a good guy."

"Yes?"

"He's … he's been touching me."

"What do you mean? I'm listening."

"On my thighs and stuff. It scared me. I told him to stop. He did for a while, but a couple days before we left for vacation, he did it again."

Sarah decides her best bet is to let Madison continue.

"I didn't want to tell you."

"Why?"

Sarah's heart is pounding.

"I don't know. Maybe I kinda liked it."

Sarah, still tapping her sandals, smiles and says, "Bobby Gardiner."

"What?"

"Bobby Gardiner. Cutest guy in freshman Spanish class. First boy to touch me more than kissing. Scared me too. But gosh, he was so cute. No boy that handsome had ever taken an interest in me."

"Bobby Gardiner?"

"Bobby Gardiner."

"So what did you do?"

"I didn't know what to do. There was no way I was going to tell my parents. They would have made an immediate phone call to a nunnery or the police. And I was too embarrassed to tell my girlfriends."

"Mom, what did you do?"

"I can still remember. You lay in your bed at night, all shocked, excited, and embarrassed at these new feelings. And at the same time not knowing if this boy giving you those feelings will be in your life next week. You feel alive, excited, happy and alone and dirty, all in the same moment."

"Mom. What. Did. You. Do?"

"Bobby had a neighbor. Tammy Blanchard. Both sets of parents started carpooling the two of them to school. Bobby and Tammy were together every morning. Suddenly, Tammy was all hot, wearing her big sister's cool clothes, and doing her makeup. I never stood a chance. Bobby handed me a note after class one day, saying he just wanted to be friends. That was the worst pain I'd ever felt. I remember thinking, 'But you said, you said!' I felt used, stupid, and ugly."

Sarah takes a chocolate out of the bag and finishes it before she speaks.

"Never told anyone what I just told you. No one. You carry stories like that inside and hope they'll go away. But like that woman on the podcast says—"

Madison finishes for her. "Unresolved issues get buried alive."

"Yeah."

"Thanks, Mom."

"For what?"

"Not freaking out on me."

"Oh, I'm freaking out. I just don't want you to see it."

"I know. I guess that's ... thank you."

"You're welcome, Madison."

"I sometimes forget you were a girl like me once."

"It was decades ago. We churned butter and used charcoal to write notes."

They both smile, still looking out at the lights.

"Mom, what do I do?"

"Well. I can tell you my first response."

"What's that?"

"We have Jeff arrested and move you into a nunnery. Too strong?"

"Yeah."

"We have to do something. Right? But at the moment, I'm not exactly sure what that is. Jeff's a good kid. Isn't he?"

"I think so, Mom. He's sure no Bobby Gardiner."

Sarah pauses a moment before asking, "Do you want to tell your dad?"

"I don't know. I know Dad loves me but there's no way we could have the talk you and I are having."

46

"Tell me about it. He's my husband. To this day I have still never told him about the time I rear-ended a parked school bus."

"You rear-ended a parked school bus?"

"No one was in it."

"A parked school bus?"

"I was looking at my phone. Next thing I know I'm getting a ticket for hitting a school bus. No way I was going to tell your father."

"A parked school bus? You're not supposed to tell me stuff like that. You're a bad influence, Mom."

Again, they both laugh into the night air.

Sarah continues, "But, I have to say, what your dad did tonight? That was a huge moment for him."

"I know."

"All right. Why don't we come back to this. Deal?"

"Deal."

"Now, let's see if we can catch up with them before your dad buys Aiden shirts we have to return."

"Thanks, Mom."

"Thank you, Madison."

Both put their sandals on and begin moving down the pier toward town. They are soon holding hands and strolling to the sound of the saxophone filling the night sky.

This is one of those exchanges when a parent can respond out of fear. And the potential of a lifelong opening will vanish into the night, just like that. Or a parent can convince his or her child he or she can handle the reality, whatever it is. In such a moment, trust and spendable, relational currency is deposited.

In what was probably only a millisecond, Sarah looked down both paths. In one very important sense, there was little choice to be made. Sarah had already made it, long before Madison risked this. A conviction prepared and formed by God for her, from before the world began.

Meanwhile, four blocks up, Aiden and his dad are struggling. They are walking through shops along Scott Street, searching for the perfect fish shirt. So far, they've found nothing. They both feel a bit lost window-shopping in overpriced boutiques.

Jim is thinking, *How hard is it to find a fish shirt? Sarah would have found the exact shirt by now.*

They're both feeling overwhelmed. Soon, they are shuffling back to the hotel. Defeated.

Neither of them has been able to talk about much, other than shirts.

This is one of those evenings where the weather and location would seem to make it perfect for a great father-and-son talk. Jim tries to jumpstart one.

"Are you having a good time on the trip?"

"I guess."

Another fifty yards of sidewalk pass under their feet.

"Anything going on in your life you'd like to talk about?"

"Like what?"

"I don't know. Life stuff."

"Stuff?"

"Yeah, life kind of stuff."

"No."

"Okay. Well if at any time on this trip you want to talk about something, I'm here."

"Okay."

"You sure there isn't anything you want to talk about?"

"Nope. No stuff. How far away is the hotel?"

"Just up the block. We're almost there."

"May I go to the pool by myself?"

"Well, I guess I can check at the front desk."

Jim realizes in this moment that nearly every communication between him and Aiden these days is superficial. It didn't used to be when Aiden was younger. When Jim had an errand to run he'd call out, "Who wants to go with me?" Aiden would yell back, "Dad, let me come!" The two would talk about everything and nothing the entire ride to the store and back.

And now, at an age when Aiden probably needs him most, Jim has no idea how to access him. The silence feels excruciating to Jim the last several hundred yards to the hotel.

Jim has never felt more like his own dad than he does tonight.

E PISODE
FIVE

A TASTE OF DISCIPLINE

The next morning the Clawsons are down on the beach in front of the Spindrift. This is Aiden's last opportunity to pretend they're a wealthy family in from Monaco, on their private yacht, circling the globe.

Having secured a late checkout, they are all now, at 1:00 p.m., showered, packed, and back in the car, heading up the coast. They are scheduled to have dinner with Jim's dad this evening, two hours ahead, in Sausalito, just north of San Francisco's Golden Gate Bridge.

They spend the first hour watching the scenery and reflecting on what they liked most about Monterey.

Eventually, Sarah turns on the next podcast. The car speakers are again carrying this now-familiar voice throughout the car.

Madison says, "Quiet, please. The parenting lady is on the air!"

"In this session, we're going to be talking about discipline."

"Hey, I thought this was about the parents, not us. Remember?"

"Hear the parenting lady out," calls Sarah.

"Yeah, quiet please, it's the parenting lady," adds Jim, smiling into the rearview mirror.

"Love without correction is permissiveness. Correction without love is punishment. Love with correction is discipline. Discipline is always for the benefit of the one being disciplined, not for the convenience of the discipliner."

"Okay, I'm listening," Madison interrupts. "Carry on, parenting lady."

"Before we unpack discipline let's talk about taste.

"There is a world of difference between disciplining a child due to harmful choices and supporting the development of a child's God-given unique tastes.

"Your children will carry unique, individual tastes, consistent with their unique make-up—music preferences, clothing styles, favorite foods, sports teams, type fonts, room decorations.

"And while emerging and maturing throughout a child's lifetime, tastes are largely neither right nor wrong, good nor evil. And so they must not be ridiculed or devalued, even if their tastes are unusual or even unpopular. When a child's tastes trigger the parent's public embarrassment, followed by demeaning the child, it's often more about the parent's immaturity than the child's.

"Parenting right and wrong is not the same as parenting tastes. Cheating or stealing or sexual immorality is not a question of taste. We have the responsibility and privilege to help clarify and show the applications of what God declares right and wrong. But parenting a child's taste is very different. We must never squash that which simply is an expression of taste just because it doesn't agree with our preference.

"Some of our children's unique gifting, talent, taste, and particular wiring are revealed through affirmation. Affirmation is giving human voice to the identification of God-developing qualities of goodness and capacity we see being expressed in another. One of the reasons we learn to affirm is to help our kids develop an accurate view of who they are and what they can and cannot do.

"Children who are not affirmed well often struggle into adulthood as they attempt to figure out who they are. Unless that affirmation is supplemented by a caring teacher, a coach, or neighbor, they can be left either bragging on who they wish they were or left insecure from who they are afraid they might be. They are left with an inaccurate view of who they are. It's never too late to begin creating a culture where this gift is given on a regular basis.

"We learn to distinguish between heart rebellion, which is brought back into healthy alignment by discipline, and heart creativity expressed in taste, which gets to be nurtured, guided, and freed. Our children are wired to deeply value our intentional engagement in both. They will ultimately appreciate discipline when it is not capricious or meant to punish. And they will never forget when you stood with them on issues of taste. Never."

Sarah turns the podcast off several minutes from the session's end as they pull into the gated community where Ray Clawson lives.

Jim lets out a deep, audible sigh. Visiting his dad makes seeing Sarah's parents seem like a complimentary wine tasting on the top deck of a cruise ship, heading leisurely for the Grand Caymans.

Jim was twelve when Ray divorced his mom. To this day, Ray is annoyed that his son can't "just get past it." For a man who sabotaged his own marriage, his dad and his endless litany of what a good marriage should look like have Jim mystified. He hypothesizes that this contributes to why no one has been willing to become Mrs. Ray Clawson for the last several decades.

Ray has created a lavish lifestyle through a remarkable capacity for buying and selling precious metals in foreign markets. His home in Sausalito overlooks the San Francisco Bay. When the fog lifts, he can see Alcatraz Island and across to Berkeley from his bedroom balcony. Ray is the epitome of the saying "money can't buy you love." He's intimidating, charismatic, rough, and unsparingly demanding. He is charming, like Vladimir Putin is charming. Most people wince at Ray's bombastic, crude, and polarizing statements. But probably, if given the chance, they'd invest their life savings in whatever he recommends.

The kids have been here once before, and they did not like it. Not one bit. Ray views children in his home like he would a homeless man with an infectious cough. Every square foot of his home is filled with the breakable and expensive spoils of conspicuous consumption. Managing kids in Ray's home is like trying to manage wet puppies inside the Louvre.

Ray's housekeeper has set the table like royalty is coming over. As the Clawsons walk out to the manicured backyard, Ray is commandeering steaks and corn on a grill. He is absolutely in his element.

Aiden is dressed in his typically eclectic attire. Whatever contemporary fashion is, Aiden has discovered a way to express nearly the opposite. The family sometimes doesn't even notice it anymore. This evening he has on what a blind man might pull out of a thrift store bin. He's wearing what looks like a referee's shirt, with sleeves hanging well below his hands, coupled with rust-colored pants, obviously cut from some bolt of burned felt. This is not a rebellion statement. It simply makes sense to him.

It doesn't make sense to Ray. Conformity makes sense to Ray. Coordinated attire makes sense to Ray. Anything else is weak, lazy, or the influence of "those left-wing intellectuals over at Berkley. Nixon should have put the kibosh on them when he had the chance."

It does not spill out until after dinner, but eventually Ray cannot help himself.

Aiden walks over to watch the sun setting onto the still standing buildings of Alcatraz prison.

Ray is seated with Jim, both of them holding a glass of Scotch. Jim hates Scotch. Ray knows Jim hates Scotch. Ray reasons that real men drink Scotch. And it's never too late for his son to become more of a man.

Ray stares at Aiden, then back to Jim. He says, loudly enough for Aiden and everyone in the family to hear, "Why does he dress like that?"

Jim responds, "What?"

"The boy. He looks like a damned pansy."

Ray points at Madison.

"Now see. His sister knows how to dress. I'm telling you, other kids are gonna make fun of him. I don't get it. Why don't you two tell him how ridiculous he looks?"

All the Clawsons are frozen in place.

"Stay a few more hours in the morning and let me take him shopping. He's not really a terrible looking kid. He just needs a decent haircut and some real clothes."

Jim quickly looks over to Aiden. Aiden turns long enough to meet his dad's eyes. It's clear he has heard his grandfather's words.

You could count on no fingers how many times Jim has stood up to his dad.

Fragments of the words Jim heard earlier come flooding over him: *"Tastes are largely neither right nor wrong, good or evil. And so they must never be ridiculed or devalued. ... We must never squash that which simply is an expression of taste just because it doesn't agree with our preference."*

Jim puts down the glass of Scotch. He wipes his mouth with the cloth napkin sitting next to his hand.

He stands, looks directly into his father's eyes and says, "Dad, thank you for the meal. We're all tired. Goodnight."

Jim nods for Aiden and the others to follow, and then turns to go.

Ray tries to say something, but Jim turns back and interrupts him. "And I still don't like Scotch. I hate Scotch."

Within less than a minute, his father's house is lit by the reflection of their Subaru's taillights.

Everybody's quiet for the next several minutes. Then Jim looks into the rearview mirror and says, "Aiden."

Aiden looks up at his father's face in the mirror, visible only by reflected dashboard light.

"Aiden, you are one of the coolest kids ever. You are kind and sensitive. You see what few of the rest of us see."

He lets that sink in before he says his next words.

"Your grandfather is wrong. Completely wrong. You dress the way you want. If kids make fun of you, it's because they don't have the creativity or uniqueness to do anything differently than the crowd. In the meantime, we've got your back."

He lets those words sink in too.

"One day you'll find a group of friends who see life like you do. And you'll probably own a clothing line that will make you rich and allow your mother and me to live on a beach in Florida."

He looks back at Aiden, who is not taking his eyes off his dad's.

"Aiden, I'm so proud you're my son."

The car is quiet again. No more words spoken, by anyone, not even the parenting lady.

Madison is beaming the entire ten-mile drive back to the hotel.

Sarah reaches over to Jim and rests her hand on his arm.

It may not be easy to know the exact moment when a family begins to find itself. But this one would be on the list.

INSIDE THE EPISODE

We just watched a parent wonderfully protect his child through the challenges of developing personal tastes. Too many battles are waged over what appears to be an issue of wrong and right when it is simply the revealing of taste.

But what about when behavior issues are not about taste, but willfully wrong choices?

Discipline is a marvelous, freeing gift of God when it is distinguished from expedience, winning, or punishment.

Nothing we ever do toward our children should ever be about any form of punishment. The purpose of discipline—and this is crucial—is to bring children back into the life-giving parameters of who they are. So, children's ability to perform pales in comparison to the development of their person.

Okay, here's the mother of all parenting verses that has unfortunately been skewered from pulpits for years. If you've not heard it directly, you've heard some variation on the theme. "Train up a child in the way he should go; even when he is old he will not depart from it" (Proverbs 22:6).

That phrase "in the way" carries the idea of parenting toward a child's particular unique personality and makeup. Not our particular personality or what the religious culture deems "the right way." God has created each of us magnificently and perfectly unique. Our responsibility and privilege, as parents, is to get in touch with our children's uniqueness so that we can guide them and direct them uniquely into God's way. The promise is, if we'll take the time to get in touch with our children's uniqueness and guide them, when they're older they won't depart from our instruction. God's heart will make sense to them, because they were given His will within their unique personality and way of learning. They will grow to be fully in touch with who they really are in God's plan. They won't have to rebel against God, or us, because they won't feel forced into an arbitrary mold that does not fit.

God knows every child's unique make-up. He created it, distinct from everyone else on this planet. To discover this demands that we stay close to our children, close enough to learn together what traps and holds down our children in destructive patterns. And close enough to learn what frees and releases the full expression of their unique bent.

Discipline is employed as a corrective, to bring children back to their unique, healthiest expression. It's helping them get back on their track.

Discipline can take many forms. It is always course correcting, helping them rethink and retrust God and others as they live through new and ongoing life challenges.

In fact, as our children grow, the best discipline doesn't always look like discipline at all. For example, it could be initiating a long drive to give them time and clarity to rethink their choice, without the shame of being called out in front of an audience.

Sometimes discipline looks like communicating to our children our own similar issues.

Many of us are afraid we're giving our kids permission to sin when we tell them the failures and wrong choices from our youth. In reality, we are powerfully blessing them, not leaving them vulnerable to sin. Especially when we can express the consequences of those choices.

Our children are left vulnerable when we pretend that we did not struggle with what they struggle with.

What valuable tools we give to our children when we not only tell them of the failure, but express who helped bring us back home! Who loved us enough to do that? Who stood with us? Who stands with us now? Our kids need to hear it all. They need to know that we know them and their real struggles. They need to know that we can relate and have already suffered consequences they do not need to.

Sometimes discipline looks like allowing our children to help in deciding the appropriate consequence for their wrong choices.

Sometimes discipline involves restricting a privilege or withholding an opportunity because they are choosing not to allow us to protect them. They need a consequence loud and constraining enough to give them a chance to catch their breath and return to their God-given design.

Sometimes, especially when children are younger, discipline might involve time-outs. Time-outs are valuable when there is a clear explanation of what you are trying to accomplish. Otherwise, the time-out may be only because the parent is out of control. There are dangerous transactions going on inside children's heads when they know they are being worked by a parent. They may accommodate you. But inside, where you may never see, they may be learning to not trust you, or the God who apparently gave you such an arbitrary technique.

Sometimes discipline can feel punitive to your child, as you are forced to keep them from an environment or group of friends who are putting them in danger. To enter into this pain and help explain your motive while they rediscover what health can look like is one of the most important times for a parent and child to find each other.

And then there will be those times when discipline will be wrongly received as punishment, no matter how well you enact it. This is why parents get more gray hairs than non-parents.

Hebrews 12 tells us love has to be the motivation for all discipline. This means I will rarely say no without a reason. "Because I said so" is not discipline but often the response of a lazy parent who simply wants to win and control but may eventually lose the heart of the child they long to influence.

Discipline is not a parental method to use when angry or out of control. This is why we spent so much time earlier in the book discussing the need for parents to face, resolve, heal, and mature through their life issues and wounding.

Objectivity is at the center of healthy parenting. It is gained through resolving life issues. Objectivity is the ability to respond to an issue and give direction to another person without it being clouded by overreaction. Before we respond to any discipline issue with our children, we must first ask, "God, have I given this to You, to reform my response in clarity and bring me to objectivity?" Then we must have the integrity to wait for it to happen. This is very hard and often requires a lot of time. And sometimes we are forced to make a decision even before our ducks are forming rows. But very few things can harm our children more than subjective overresponse in their vulnerable moment of need. Objectivity is one of the finest gifts we can offer our children.

Here are two scenarios to consider: (a) when our child gets hurt, and (b) when our child hurts someone.

The remedy for when our child gets hurt is real forgiveness.

There is a type of false forgiveness we might try to evoke, because it can temporarily give the illusion of covering over the situation. But it creates only resentment and never allows for the hurt one to get unhurt. The formula sounds like this: "Now, Bobby, because we are Christians, we are supposed to forgive that boy who hit you. Now, let's do that. Tell Cameron you forgive him. See now, don't we feel better?"

No, Bobby does not feel better. He feels betrayed and worked by his parent. He may be able to move on in the moment, but he is left with resentment and no way to get free of it. Bobby is about to descend down a course of harboring bitterness for an act he can't get vindication for. The healing was cut off at the pass. It drives him absolutely crazy and soon makes him the issue, becoming the victim twice. Bobby is forced into self-protection that can take the form of gossip, jealousy, or outbursts of unrelated anger. Such parental manipulation sounds like a perfect religious methodology. But it only confuses and grates on our kids until they mistrust this God who would have created such an unjust formula.

What Bobby and every one of us needs when we get hurt is a way to no longer have to be in charge of enacting justice for ourselves. We are simply not created for it. Only God can be our vindicator.

Now the remedy for when my child hurts another is real repentance.

As with the above, there is a type of false apology/repentance we often evoke. But again, it's false, so it achieves nothing true. The formula sounds like this: "Now Bobby, you have done something wrong. You must repent. Promise God and us that you will not do this again. Okay? Let's repent. See now, Bobby, don't we feel better?"

No, Bobby does not feel better. He feels betrayed and played. He feels guilted into a bankrupt religious formula forcing him to be a liar to God. It may eventually make him anesthetized to the voice and wooing of God. The worst-case scenario is that Bobby grows up to be one very angry dude.

What Bobby and every one of us need when we hurt another is a way to no longer be forced to buck up and make a promise animated only by the flesh instead of Christ in us.

Few experiences as a parent are more gratifying than being trusted to help walk your child through real forgiveness and real repentance.

You will be changing generational patterns and freeing children in future generations, ones you may never meet in this lifetime. By the same token, few experiences as a parent are more gut-wrenching. Walking with your child through real forgiveness and real repentance will call on all your reserves as a parent. But remember, we don't have to do this by ourselves. We are not alone. We have Christ in us.

Up ahead we have much more to say about real forgiveness and repentance.

BACK TO EPISODE 5: A TASTE OF DISCIPLINE

Today is the vacation's turnaround point. Tomorrow the Clawsons will begin their journey home. But today they are in San Francisco! They visit Ghirardelli Square. They eat lunch at Fisherman's Wharf. Then they ride cable cars and drive down Lombard Street. And yes, they pay homage to the Old Fillmore West. Jim's mom wouldn't forgive them if they didn't. As a teenager, one magical summer evening in 1970, she saw Jimi Hendrix, Cream, and The Paul Butterfield Blues Band in a single concert at the Fillmore!

As the afternoon sun begins to retreat behind the skyscrapers, the Clawsons park their car near AT&T park where the San Francisco Giants play. They make the considerable walk through Battery Park and Chinatown all the way to Little Italy. There, they attempt to track down Firenze by Night, reputed to have the best chicken parmesan in the area. Jim would steal money for good chicken parmesan. The late afternoon sun is painting the tops of the buildings orange and yellow in the Embarcadero District as they climb the hill leading to the restaurant.

Firenze is what you'd expect from an indigenous, family-owned restaurant in the heart of Little Italy. A white-shirted man named Gaspare, who seems to know everyone, treats the Clawsons like they are nightly regulars. Gaspare pours wine into glasses at each table, whether they particularly want it or not. He leans into the Clawsons, darting a glance over his shoulder, as though he's telling a secret. He whispers, "We've been saving this wine for a special occasion. Tonight, my friends, we open it for you." It's a delightful lie he repeats at nearly every table.

"Mom," Madison calls out over the din. "May Aiden and I go out front until dinner comes? We want to check out some of the shops."

"Stay near the restaurant. Be back in ten minutes."

"Yep."

Madison and Aiden walk back out through the entrance onto the street. Suddenly the air is wildly alive. Restaurateurs merge with small retail merchants and well-dressed businessmen and women. An old Asian man hauls produce with a handcart in one direction while two shirtless men are carrying a sofa over their heads in the other. No one in the crowd sharing the sidewalk even seems to notice. Humanity just merges and shifts. It's loud, chaotic, brightly humming, and a bit scary.

Madison and Aiden have not seen anything quite like it before.

They stop about a half block from the restaurant in front of an appliance showroom. They find a pocket of space under the store's awning, an arm's length from the crowd, flowing by like a river. The lights of the storefronts are just now coming on.

Madison and Aiden are staring straight ahead out at the street of loud and electric buzz. The two of them are feeling very independent, like they are both very much part of this city scene.

"You don't see this in Scottsdale," Madison says, above the street noise.

"Nope," Aiden answers.

"Look, I just want to tell you that even though you're my brother, you're pretty cool. I do think you wear really weird clothes. But Coley Brady thinks you look good."

"Coley Brady?"

"Yeah. She said, 'Your brother knows how to be himself. I like that.'"

"She said that? Coley Brady said that?"

"Yep. Coley. Brady."

She lets the words play out slowly.

"I think you know how to be yourself too. I like that."

Aiden breaks the stare and looks over at his sister. She lets her stare remain fixed, staring at a man across the street banging on plastic buckets with drumsticks.

Moments later they begin their way back to the restaurant.

When the grace of God invades a family, all manner of goodness begins to appear. Grace is not only how each of the Trinity relates

59

to each other, but how God wants to relate with us. It's also how He longs for us to relate to each other. Because of the cross, we no longer have to interact with each other in fear, comparisons, condemnation, hidden resentments, or even impressive accomplishment. We are loved, cherished, and endlessly valued.

One of the indicators that grace is beginning to invade a family's DNA is in what we just witnessed. The Clawson kids are increasingly able to honor and affirm each other. They will still fight and get on each other's nerves. They will still complain in the back seat about the smell of the other's shoes. But they are learning to protect each other and make sure the other knows they are enough to make it.

Another gift of grace is that less is done from the script of parental role and authority. Some parents are afraid to be themselves around their kids for fear they won't be respected or obeyed. So they think every story must have a moral, every event a teaching moment. And every emotion must have a cap, a sanitized lid. The kids end up knowing only an idealized caricature of their parents.

Tonight, Jim and Sarah have fewer filters. Sarah is telling stories about the first time Jim took her out on a date. Jim sings too loudly during their long walk back to the car. At one point, this Friday evening throng along the sidewalk gets so congested and loud that Madison finds herself taking her dad's arm. It surprises him. Instinctively, he stands taller as they wait at the intersection. He's not felt this way in a long time.

Then, without warning, pretending he's a celebrity, Jim shouts out a facetious rebuke to the crowd at the intersection: "Please, people. I've told you before! No pictures when I'm with my family. Please respect that." He's done this bit before. Too many times. But this time, Madison is barely embarrassed. She continues to hold his arm as the light turns green and the crowd moves on.

Sarah, watching from behind, smiles and stands taller too.

E PISODE
SIX

THE HEART OF THE
MATTER

Jim's mom, Allison, lives in Groveland, a little over two hours from San Francisco.

Groveland has fewer than seven hundred residents. Allison likes it that way. Though she raised Jim and his two brothers with Ray in Sausalito before the divorce, she never fit into that culture. She's always been a bit of a hippie. She now lives in a small but comfortably eclectic home behind Dori's Tea Cottage. Dori's sits prominently alongside several other establishments on Main Street, a few miles from the entrance to Yosemite National Park.

Jim had just turned twelve when Ray left Allison.

Ray had an affair. Actually, Ray had a number of affairs. He just got caught in the last one.

Allison then quickly moved Jim and his two brothers to Sacramento. Only two years ago, after all the boys had started their families elsewhere, Allison finally sold the house and moved up here.

It is said that divorce takes two. Sometimes it only takes the selfishness, wounding, and immaturity of one. Then it wildly affects

61

two, and all they have in the world—their children, friends, parents, neighbors, and extended community.

This divorce was one of those.

Allison is a magnificent mom. She was an excellent wife. She did not deserve her marriage to end this way, inadvertently discovering a series of brazen messages on a voicemail machine from someone named Carla.

Jim loves his mom deeply. He has been so looking forward to this reunion.

Sarah also loves and delights in Allison. She confides in her more than she does her own mom.

And as for Madison and Aiden, this visit is maybe the most anticipated stop along the trip.

The Clawsons pull into Groveland around ten in the morning. Allison's home is like something out of a scene from *The Hobbit*. Lush green slopes surround her old but sturdy stone home. The roof is covered in cedar shake wooden shingles. The inside is appointed like a rustic antique store where nothing is for sale. There are black and white pictures everywhere. Several driftwood-framed oil paintings depict visited ocean coves. Candles and incense appear to be perpetually burning. Tapestries cover walls. The floors are polished cedar and wonderfully creaky. The colors and lighting are deep, rich, and warm. Everything is eclectically artistic but tastefully cool. You could sleep through the night in any of the leather chairs and couches throughout this tiny but exceedingly comfortable home.

"Wow!" Aiden mouths before he can actually say the word. "This place is awesome, Grandma!"

Allison would have always decorated like this. But when married to a controller, the other person's tastes and preferences most often win out. And if a person is not a fighter, creativity is gradually shut down and that particular expression of the person. Allison was not a fighter. So she spent those years teaching the children her values, amidst his tastes.

Allison was, during those years, a very competent and sought-after radio station manager in the Bay area. She chose to put all that on hold until all the children were out of her home.

These days she makes the trek down the hill into Stockton three days a week to help a fledgling radio station. They primarily broadcast music from the '60s and '70s and intersperse the sets with interviews, catching up with the artists' current lives. It's all very unpolished, unedited, and highly listened to. NPR carries several of their segments.

She answers Aiden, "You like this old place? Aww! That makes your grandma so happy. You might have some hippie in you, kid!"

Everyone laughs. It is safe and knowing laughter.

Jim and his mom have talked about the divorce many times. But he continues to form more questions as he grows older. Especially this time, after having seen Ray.

He wonders often how his mom, who was so deeply wounded and wronged, is so vitally healthy, while Ray, who still appears to be the winner, is filled with so much twisted, arrogant ugliness.

This evening everyone picks through platters of meats, cheeses, breads, and hummus, all spread out on Allison's giant patio table, interspersed with a huge display of colorful vegetables and fruits from her own garden.

Aiden and Madison light dozens of candles for Allison and the smoke of several sticks of cinnamon incense drifts in the background. The patio is as comfortable as the living room.

The kidney-shaped table faces west. At over three thousand feet, her patio gives the illusion they are looking down on the setting sun in the immense valley, stretching all the way to the Pacific Ocean.

After sitting silently long enough to drink in this moment, Allison stands to reach for the bottle of red wine several feet down the table. Then she rearranges her long, flowing peasant skirt, and gracefully sits back down.

"Well, first I just want to say how good it feels to have you all at this table. I've sat out here many evenings, imagining what this would feel like. And it is better than I could picture. Aiden, you and I have much to talk about. You have an artist's eye, pal! Madison, I am so curious about what you're interested in. Your mom has asked if you and I could spend some time together on Skype. I think that would be so cool."

"I think that would be cool too, Grandma." Madison smiles from the end of the table. "I was the one who asked Mom if we could do that."

"Well then, everyone, enjoy. There are blankets if it gets too cold. Anything you'd like, if it's not out here, is either on the kitchen counter or in the refrigerator. You don't need to ask. This is your home."

Bright reddish-orange fills the entire sky behind Allison.

Everyone is entering in. Even Aiden. Maybe especially Aiden. Spontaneous laughter, questions, unhurried answers. Stories. Everyone is getting their chance to be heard.

Jim has been thinking a lot about tonight. Next Thursday is his mom's sixty-third birthday. He and Sarah and the kids have prepared an album filled with photos and memorabilia from his childhood, along with pictures of her with Madison and Aiden when they were little. She's going to love it.

He also wants to thank her in front of his kids. Jim has so much he wants to say. Each day on this trip has increasingly deepened his appreciation for what an incredible parent she has been all these years.

"So, Mom, we just visited Dad."

Aiden speaks for the entire family: "Why did you ever marry him? The guy is a jerk."

Allison laughs—that unguarded laughter, which signals to all that there are no secrets or land mines to fear.

"Yes, he can be, my dear. Yes, he can."

After dishes are cleared from the table, Sarah and Madison emerge from the kitchen with a lit birthday cake.

"Sorry, Grandma," Madison says. "They didn't have sixty-three candles at the store. You'll have to be twenty-four tonight. That's how many candles come in a pack. And they only had one."

"Well, tonight I feel twenty-four. Thank you all. Please don't sing. I hate when people sing that song. I always have. And I'm old enough to have my way."

She blows out the candles to applause.

Glasses are refilled, cake is cut and passed around.

Then, Jim's moment has arrived.

"Ahem." He sighs as though he may not be able to continue.

"Mom, I've told you this before. But on this occasion, I want to remind you again—to have my wife and children hear this. So, here goes. You tried to tell me about Jesus. But I wanted nothing to do with Him. I was so angry. At everything. I missed our huge house. I missed my friends. I missed the neighbor's daughter, Sheri Phillips. I missed everything. I blamed you for taking us to Sacramento."

Sarah interrupts. "Wasn't this going to be a birthday affirmation?"

"I'm getting there."

He stands up. He pulls out a piece of paper and begins reading.

"But you kept loving us. And that's exactly what we needed. You kept doing what two parents would do, by yourself. You kept our family together. You kept showing me Jesus, even though I didn't want anything to do with Him. You kept convincing me life would turn out well if I wouldn't give up. You kept praying over me. You were so strong with me, so kind to me. You taught me what was right and what was wrong and why. You wouldn't let me get away with self-entitled permission to do wrong. I'll never forget when a bunch of us kids took Mr. Wilkin's goat on a prank. You made us take it back and clean up his barn. For parts of four weekends! But that first night, before we returned the goat, you made us sleep in the backyard with him. Who does that? But you always sat with me when you did something like that, explaining why you were doing what you were doing.

"You told me ridiculously wrong things you did as a teenager, and you didn't make it sound fake or religious. And you told me what was fun about it. Then you told me why you regretted it, who you hurt, and who walked you through the damage you did. You gradually gave me more of a voice into how I would be parented. You made me understand the options when I just wanted you to give me a rule or a one-liner. You taught me to obey when I wanted to rebel. You kept prying, asking, and finding a way in. You asked great questions. All the time with the questions. Questions that forced me to ask good questions of my life.

"As I got older I still needed you to keep telling me who I was, what I was good at, what I wasn't as good at. You listened to my pain and anger, no matter how rudely and arrogantly it came out. You kept affirming my right to be angry. You helped me cry. You helped me take it to God, even though I didn't really want to talk to Him then. I never told you, but I loved those moments when you did that. You shared your anger and your pain. You let me see you cry. You let me see you be irrational. You let us hold you when you were beyond exasperated.

"You made up ridiculous games for us to play at the dinner table.

You dressed in silly costumes at holidays. And you made sure we saw when you dressed up for dates or nights out with friends, to show us you had not lost your dignity or beauty. You kept taking us back to Monterey so we'd realize we were still a family. You convinced us we weren't a loser family. That God had a future for us, even in our brokenness.

"You kept convincing us that you still had a great life. You taught my brothers to want to take me places and talk to me about stuff you couldn't. You surrounded me with good men who would take me for walks and drives and ball games, to offer me father figures. Because you knew I needed a dad.

"I needed you to believe in me. And you did. You were almost always in my business. But you knew when to leave me alone.

"Somehow you came to almost every game. And even more importantly, you let me see when you just couldn't do any more. You didn't hide it from me.

"You let me know that you hated being alone and without a husband.

"It wasn't until college that I opened up to Jesus. I was just so hurt.

"I'm discovering that I haven't known how to show this faith to my kids like you showed it to me. I'm discovering how much I haven't known how to trust Jesus with my own life. These last ten days have shown me that.

"Happy birthday, Mom! I still need you. We still need you. Love, Jim."

He walks over to where Allison is seated. She stands up and they hug each other, for a long moment.

She then steps back enough to place her hands on his shoulders and says, "Thank you, Jim. I could not possibly have asked for a better birthday gift. And yes, I would be so honored to learn together with all of you how to live this life in Christ. For the rest of my days."

Aiden starts the applause and all join in.

Then Jim and Aiden make their way to the fire ring near the table and prepare a fire. Jim rearranges chairs and passes out blankets. Allison brings out a tray of hot chocolate. Soon, the conversations move from cake frosting, to why we can still see stars that no longer exist, to bands who played the Fillmore, to why park rangers wear those stiff-brimmed hats with the tassels.

At some point, Jim asks the question on everyone's mind: "Mom, how in the world did you ever learn to forgive Dad?"

She furrows her brow at Jim for an uncomfortably long time. Then suddenly she calmly takes in the faces around the fire.

"I hated your father. For what he did to me. For what it would do to you and your brothers. For months and months I could feel that the bitterness was crippling me. He was able to hurt me twice. First, by violating me and our marriage. And then by going on like nothing happened while I sunk steadily into this deep, deep darkness. Um, are you all sure you are up for this?"

Everyone is hoping their particular facial expression is giving her the confidence to continue.

"So you were twelve, Jim. I don't know exactly what you remember."

Jim responds, "I remember Dad yelling a lot. He'd been found out and he was blaming you. Like if you had been more attractive, or knew more about business, or kept a neater home, or whatever, he wouldn't have had to have an affair. I knew he was all wrong. I just didn't know what to say. I would usually just leave the house. I'm so sorry."

"Jim, you don't ever have to be sorry. You were twelve. Think about that—twelve. I think that is one of the horrible collateral damages of a parent's sin. The child keeps thinking, all through their lives, that they could have, should have done more. You have been a wonderful son. None of that was your fault. Do you understand me?"

She reaches over to him and puts her hand on his arm.

"Anyway, that's when Jesus happened to this hippie."

"What do you mean, Grandma?" asks Aiden.

She leans back and laughs. "Jesus. And Helen Cacoris. Okay, let's see, where to start. When we moved to Sacramento, I felt so alone in my shame and self-isolation. But there was a dear older lady from across the street who began inviting herself over. She seemed so odd and overly kind at first. She would just show up with carafes of coffee and plates of scones. At first I dreaded it when I'd hear that knock on the door. I just wanted to close the drapes and be left alone. Many times I didn't answer. But she kept coming by. When I did let her in, mostly she just listened. You were all in school and

I was out of work. I was lost. Totally, freaked-out lost. Just to have her listen to me was everything.

"Helen Cacoris. Kindly, gently, and patiently, she waited me out. When she finally did tell me about Jesus, I was ready. She'd proven she was there to love me, not sell me something. I was drawn to Him like a moth to light. Love like I'd never seen. Hope. Life bigger than my loss. He's the love that singers back in my day were trying to imagine. They didn't just sing about relationships back then. They were writing about trying to find God. Richie Havens. I can remember him trying so hard to get it out in lyrics. You know, he later became a Christian."

She stares off for a bit. Then she regroups and says, "Sorry. I got a bit lost there. I did do some drugs back in the early days."

Everyone smiles, but quickly locks back in, not wanting to lose one moment in the story.

"After I started believing in Jesus, I felt so much better. Like I would make it. But I was still bitter.

"One day Helen said, 'You know, Allison, you must forgive Ray.' She may as well have said, 'Allison, I think you should macramé a refrigerator magnet from shards of gypsum.' There was no way I could forgive him. I hated him for what he did to us.

"I remember that exact day. Helen excused herself. I was overwhelmed with a sense I would suffocate if I didn't get outside. Moments later, I'm standing in the backyard, gasping out these words: 'I'm so tired, Jesus. Helen's right. I'm bitter. I'm angry and full of revenge. God, I love You. But I've been so afraid to give You what I've carried. It feels like, if I give up my rights to it, I will lose me. Like I'd be giving up my chance to be vindicated, shown to be right, shown to be worth loving. I fear You might not come through. And then what would I do? But I'm done. I surrender, Jesus. I forgive Ray. You be the judge and jury for everything Ray has done. Everything.'

"It probably wasn't nearly that articulate. I think I've embellished it over the years.

"Then I laid down in the yard and wept and wept and wept. It was probably hours later that your brother Andy came home and noticed me sprawled on the ground. He ran and knelt down next to me and asked, 'Mom, what's wrong? Are you okay?'

"I slowly sat up on the grass and took his hand. I told him, 'Andy, I think we're going to be okay. I think we're going to be okay.'"

Allison puts her hands in her lap. Her mouth is open, like she has more to say. But what she's said is enough.

INSIDE THE EPISODE

So many of our attempts at forgiveness leave us frustrated, resentful, wounded, cynical. Basically, we're still trapped in our unforgiveness. It's largely because we have an incomplete understanding of forgiveness. First, it may surprise us that forgiveness has an order. We saw earlier that we initiate a vertical transaction with God before we can move into a horizontal forgiveness with another. The vertical transaction forgives my offender before God, for my benefit. This is not excusing any action.

In other words, when I get hurt, it can feel like God is not moving fast enough to vindicate me. The offender is going on without missing a beat, and I'm left holding the bag. Somewhere back there in that distortion of jilted pain, I can make the decision that God was either unable or unwilling to protect me sufficiently. No longer believing that God was perfectly, in His own timing, protecting me, vindicating me, and wanting to carry my case, I can decide to defend myself. That's when the hooks, the crippling consequences of not trusting Jesus with me, become embedded deep in my entire being. The wounded victim now becomes doubly wounded by the effects of carrying sin done against me. I become the issue.

From that moment on, I begin to lose my objectivity, perspective, and joy.

I begin to take things into my own hands and build my own case. I move from trusting God's ability to defend me to imagining I can and must be judge and jury myself. Jesus died for every sin because I am not capable of handling any sin without getting very sick. God says He protects the humble, but He has to sit on His hands until my prideful, self-protecting self gets tired enough to let Him take over. Until that happens I hold on to every wrong and carry them around. Eventually they weigh me down, and I become bitter, self-absorbed, and full of blame.

So God waits until I become tired or sick or I miss His friendship enough. As much as He wants to rush in to protect me, this is one area where He must wait for me to trust Him with all of this. He is waiting for my trust and humility. I must agree with Jesus that I cannot carry this. I choose to let go of being judge and jury. I tell God I am sorry for believing He was not sufficiently able or willing to take care of me. Then I can intentionally give Him permission to carry all that I have been miserably attempting to bear.

In that truly miraculous moment, the hooks begin to come out. God is revealed as completely willing and able to protect me.

This is the miraculous, maybe as powerful as anything we get to see in this age.

I will know I've trusted God for a vertical forgiveness when I no longer need to have my offender grovel and give the "perfect" apology to the entire world, on worldwide television! I will know the hooks are out when I want to approach my offender in love, to give the opportunity for a horizontal forgiveness (based on repentance) for their benefit. This will not always be practically possible. But it can become the deep desire of my heart. This is how love works. I am completely freed as I trust that God is able to protect, release, and heal me. Then, with nothing else left to self-protect, I am able to love for the benefit of those who have wronged me. This is where this faith in our God becomes immensely real. This is love others are stunned by. Because it can't be faked, at least not for very long. It is truly a work of God.

BACK TO EPISODE 6: THE HEART OF THE MATTER

Jim asks his mom, "Have you ever been able to talk to him about that? About forgiveness, about Jesus, about what it's all doing to him?"

"Jim, your father is a very stubborn, proud man. In a strange way, it is probably the reason why he has made so much money. But it came with a cost. 'Jesus is for uneducated, weak people,' he says. We are civil, even at times playful with each other. I have no fight in me for him. I sometimes still like the man! Look, if there were no him, there wouldn't be you and your brothers. I've tried a dozen times to give him a chance to see his failure so he can repent and own his mess. So he could let God cleanse him. So he could hear me forgive him for it all, to be free of it all."

And not long after those words, everyone begins to make their way back into the house, knowing they have shared an evening none of them will soon forget.

The next morning Allison drives down the hill to the radio station in Stockton. The Clawsons have been gifted with a do-nothing day. They all sleep in, which for them is about 7:15 a.m. They unhurriedly do laundry, take long showers, and catch up with e-mails and social media. Aiden tries out each of the chairs and couches. Allison gave him permission to play her vinyl albums. She showed him how to put the needle to the record without scratching it. Most of the day he is trying out different incenses while loudly playing everything from Dylan to The Grateful Dead to John Coltrane. Eventually Madison and Sarah make the short walk to try out Dori's Tea Cottage. Jim takes his computer outside to catch up with the home office.

The rest of the day is uneventful. This trip has been a whirlwind. This vacation has turned into more of an extended field trip of discovery. A family discovering itself. Today everyone feels its weight. Each of them just needs a chance to get away and be alone for a bit. This they do all the way until bedtime.

THE ROAD TO MY HEART

Jim doesn't know everything about his kids, but he does know he connects best with Madison while they're walking together.

So the next morning he invites her on a hike to explore the hills out back of Allison's home. She's a little skittish, but she agrees. They join a logging road and soon are surrounded by dense forest. This is exactly what they were hoping for. In their daypacks they have plenty of water and some of last evening's leftovers.

Jim is starting to realize how much his approach to parenting has been screwed up by his dad. Ray has always just won. Everyone does it his way, because his way is right—even when he is wrong. So, while others might accommodate or comply with Ray, no one actually trusts him. Seeing his mom so soon after Ray has really stunned Jim.

Today Jim wants his relationship with Madison to change.

"Madison, your mom says you two had a really good talk back in Monterey."

"What did she tell you?"

"No details. Just that it was good."

"Yeah."

They continue walking. Jim is fairly sure Madison will tell him about it if given a little time.

Jim is wrong.

Madison says nothing. For over ten minutes of walking.

They finally take a break to drink from their water bottles.

"So, would you like to talk to me about what you talked about?"

"No, Dad. I don't think so."

Madison has capped her water bottle and begun walking again.

A truth about trust and permission from an earlier podcast:

> "If you are seeking permission to talk about a particular subject and the answer is no, it would be a good idea to honor that no until, at some point in the future, a yes is secured."

Jim is about to steamroll this particular piece of counsel.

"Why does your mom get to know things that I don't? I'm your dad."

She keeps walking.

"Madison," he calls ahead, more loudly than he needs to.

She stops. And turns.

"Dad. No."

"No, what? I'd just like to know what you were talking about. Stop making it such a big deal like it was some mysterious secret."

Almost to herself, but loud enough for him to hear, Madison says, "Was this your plan?"

He moves in front of where she is staring. "What? My plan? Don't you trust me?"

"No. I don't."

"Why can't you trust me? I don't even know what you mean when you say that."

"That's why I don't trust you."

"Stop saying that! You can't just say that because you want to. I'm trustworthy! I'm faithful to your mom. I take care of you. I'm honest. I don't get why you keep saying that."

"Mom listens. And she doesn't go all nuts on me. She doesn't use it as permission to tell me what's wrong with me or how I'm doing it all wrong."

He's indignant. "I don't agree with that at all. I listen."

"You're so afraid I'm going to screw up my life. I don't even hear you anymore. I just tune you out."

This is not the first time they've had this particular conversation. But something is different this time.

Even though he's overreacting, Jim is allowing Madison to be truthful. He's confused, frustrated, angry. But he chooses to let Madison get it out. He can't yet have any idea how much there is to get out.

They both sit on some rocks near the edge of the road. Madison turns to look at him.

"Dad. Don't you think that I might know just about everything I *shouldn't* do by now? I'm fourteen. Why do you want to keep telling me ten more times? I'm not deaf."

"I don't know what to say."

"Why couldn't we have just hiked, and maybe you ask how I'm doing, or how I'm feeling?"

"Apparently I don't know."

"You treat me like I can't be trusted. And so you don't ever get to see when I get it right. I keep waiting for you to just tell me when you see I'm getting it right. Just once. But you don't trust me, so I don't trust you."

"Madison, I'm just afraid that—"

"I know, Dad. So why would I ever tell you anything really important about my life? I know how you'll react."

"This isn't fair. I'm trying to raise you to be a healthy young woman."

She rolls her eyes. "Oh my god. I'm angry most of the time. Do you know that? And you would not want to know the thoughts I have."

"Okay. Enough. So what do you want me to do?"

She looks into his eyes. She's staring to see how much she will pay for being truthful.

"Dad. Ask about my life. Everything's changing. And I don't know what to do most of the time. I'd like to know you cared."

"Madison—"

"Let me talk! I'm messing up and don't even know who to tell. Tell me you messed up too. Dad, I know what the right thing is. I've heard it from you five thousand times. But I don't know how to do it."

She is crying now.

"I'm an idiot," Jim confesses.

"Don't make it about you, Dad. Make it about me."

They sit there for some time.

Jim awkwardly breaks the silence. "Let's just hike. No questions."

So they do. A long hike. Until both of them are very tired.

For this day, it is more than enough.

Today Jim learned something he has never before considered. If he is ever going to earn Madison's trust, if he is ever going to be given permission into anything, he must do it in a counterintuitive way. By vulnerability, not power. By seeking permission.

On this day, Madison may have given her dad a way home.

INSIDE THE EPISODE

We just watched Jim trying to demand permission. Yeah, no bueno. He has presumed that because he is Madison's father, he has the right to the issues of her heart. But Jim is just now beginning to learn a vital truth that will eventually shape the entire trajectory of his parenting.

Permission to the heart is earned. Always.

Anyone can give you information, even knowledge. They are simple receptions of your mind. You don't have to trust me to give you information. It happens all the time. An obnoxious phone solicitor can tell you what time it is. You don't have to trust that person's motives in order to receive it.

Sadly, this is why many churches put a premium on biblical information over biblical transformation. Because the first takes only a position of authority and distribution of materials. Biblical information is indispensably important, but by itself it is grossly insufficient. Under such a system, you can become convinced you are a "successful" Christian because you know a lot about the Bible. But the Christian faith is endlessly more than knowing things about God.

As Paul says in Philippians 3:10 (NIV), "I want to know Christ." (The Greek word for "know," *ginosko*, shouts out my ability to experientially know Jesus!) There needs to be a means to turn information into transformation. Knowledge must be allowed to turn into truth, wisdom, insight, and discernment.

Truth that is not trusted does not transform, no matter how valuable that truth is.

The implications of this for me as a parent are endless. For in wanting to love and influence my children, I must first earn their trust.

Influence. More than anything, we want to influence our children for good. But influence cannot be forced. Influence cannot be given without permission from the one we want to influence. And permission, well, that's tricky, because it is almost an involuntary transaction on the part of our children. They cannot be coerced, demanded, or manipulated into giving us permission. Permission is a function of trust.

I want to learn what it takes to earn the trust of my children. It doesn't take sinless perfection for my children to trust me. They are hardwired to forgive me ten thousand times multiplied by infinity. What they are not hardwired for is my—wait for it—lack of integrity.

Integrity is simply doing that which you said you can do. And not promising to do what you cannot. It is the quality of being trusted to be who you say you are, and not to use your role as a parent to get what you want.

This means that you don't presume to be able to solve everything and protect everything and know everything. You are asking your children to allow you access to protect them only in areas you have the capacity to do so. Their trust of you comes largely through your humility to admit what you cannot yet be trusted for. And to be able to receive their honest reflection when you violate their trust by trying to force access in areas where you are not yet trusted.

Most kids love superheroes. But they don't want them for parents.

One of the ways your kids can tell you if they trust you to influence them is to listen carefully to their answer when you ask, "How am I affecting you?" Once they believe you sincerely want to know, you will discover the areas in which they are not allowing themselves to trust your influence.

That question—How am I affecting you?—may sound a bit strange. Not strange as in bad, but strange as in odd. But we encourage you to be a little odd in your parenting and this is a great first step. What you're essentially asking your child is, "When you're with me, do you feel free to be yourself or do you have to edit yourself?" The effect we have on our children makes them feel either free or not and, of course, sometimes it may make them feel a little of both. But be boldly odd, ask them, and see what they say.

We are employed by God to meet our children's needs as a conduit of God's protective love. And we access their hearts in the same way God has accessed ours—through trust.

It is protection, not control.

And our children will more readily give that permission to us as they see us giving it to others.

When our children trust us, they grow in freedom. It really is a beautiful thing to see.

And when such a way of interaction begins to be released in a family, children give permission willingly, not begrudgingly. Plus they'll begin to reveal more of themselves. They will feel the protection to be more vulnerable. Again, it's a beautiful thing to see.

Jim has been given a tentative invitation into Madison's heart. He's on a pretty big learning curve here, and he knows it. But he has been invited, and that's muy bueno.

BACK TO EPISODE 7: THE ROAD TO MY HEART

Meanwhile, Sarah and Allison have decided to walk over to Dori's Tea Cottage. They ask Aiden if he'll be all right by himself for a while.

"Yeah. Don't worry."

He has been waiting for them to leave. Now he has the whole hippie house to himself. As soon as they step out the door, he lights incense and puts on another album.

Seated out front, overlooking a very quiet Main Street, the two women divide a loaf of Dori's homemade olive oil-lemon bread. Allison has set them both up with a pot of loose-leaf green Kukicha tea.

Dylan's scratchy voice is faintly heard from Allison's home, directly behind them.

Allison nods her head, smiling. "That boy's got taste."

"So, how did you do it?" Sarah asks, waiting for her tea to cool.

"Do what?"

"Raise three kids by yourself? I'm having the hardest time raising two. And I have a husband."

"I think you're doing a really good job, Sarah. Tell me, how has it been, travelling all together? Everybody gets revealed a bit, riding in a car together after a while. Yes?"

"Yes, revealed 'a bit.' It's been good, but also really hard and exasperating. I'm not even sure how long we've been gone."

"So, what's the hardest for you? In parenting."

"You want me to pick just one? Sometimes everything. Earlier this week, we were down at my parents' place in Encinitas. I had to get out of the house and just walk. I felt so claustrophobic."

"I understand. I'm a card-carrying claustrophobe. So what does that mean for you?"

"I felt like I was being exposed as a fake. Like my kids could see it as they watched my mom. Like they were looking at me and wanted to say, 'So that's where you got it. A detached, hard woman who doesn't know how to love her kids, but just throws edicts at them and makes them feel guilty all the time. This is all so clear now.'"

Allison smiles. "Perhaps you were reading a bit too much into their expressions?"

Sarah smiles back. "Perhaps. But, Allison, I saw myself in her. A lot. I feel like I've been working most of my adult life trying to get her out of my system. She's not a bad person. She's done a lot of good things. I love her. *But she spent my entire childhood teaching me to appear to be good.*"

"That'll drive you to claustrophobia."

"My goal was to keep her convinced of my acceptability. That I was worth her love. So I was always performing to be enough for her. And I never was acceptable enough. I'm still not. I'm thirty-eight years old and my mom still can't keep from pointing out what I do wrong. Even when it involves children who don't belong to her! It's what her parents taught her. Now I feel like I'm doing the same thing to Madison and Aiden. We haven't talked about it on the trip. But I know it's coming. They're so on to me!"

"Crazy, huh?" Allison muses. "The older we get the more childish and caricatured our parents seem each time we visit them."

"I honestly don't know how to enjoy my kids. I do love them. But like my mom, I'm trying to fix them, make them show better. They must feel just like I have all these years. Like they're not measuring up. I want to help them grow up and live right. But how do I do that? I watch other moms and it's like they took a class I missed. It seems to come naturally."

"So, back to my question. What's the hardest for you?"

"Okay. I guess it's this: How do you get to enjoy your kids when you have to be the one to correct them all the time?"

"Ah, you are asking such good questions. So, first, let me tell you that it didn't come naturally to me. I just fell in love with Ray. I wasn't one of those girls who dreamed of children. I would have liked to have been 'a seamstress for the band.'"

"A what?"

"Sorry. Old Elton John reference." She laughs.

"You didn't want children?"

"Its not that I didn't want children, or didn't love them when they came. But, honey, I was a really good station manager. However, life comes and the next thing comes. And the next thing for me became to protect three boys. And I didn't have a clue. I was drowning just trying to survive an ugly divorce."

"I can't even imagine."

"Looking back, I can't either. I don't want to sound trite, but that's when Jesus rescued me. At first it was believing the basics about Him—that He was God and that He loved me enough to die for me. That He was always thinking about me. Then I gradually began to believe some things about me—that I wasn't this failure, this unwanted woman. That I was loved, known, and had new life inside of me. After a while I could come home from work and do more than just hold on until I could take my next sleeping pill. I could feel myself starting to come alive. I don't know how the kids survived before that. I was in a fog. But the fog started to lift and suddenly I cared deeply about my kids, about their lives, about us."

"Allison, I want that."

"You want *what*?"

"What you're saying. To experience that new life in me. For my family to experience that new life in them. I don't think that way. I don't even know what that would look like."

"I don't know when it dawned on me. For all the years before, I was just trying to get them to behave and be well adjusted, without it costing me too much. Then one day I had this thought from nearly out of nowhere: *God's Spirit is maturing me from the inside out, even when I don't notice it. Even when I'm not awake! So, maybe He's doing the same with my kids.*

"That single thought changed so much in my parenting! I started trying to appeal to God in them instead of running around all day trying to manage their behavior."

"Help me, Allison. What does that even mean, 'appeal to God in them'?"

Allison smiles. "Yes. That. Well, I kept reminding them and teaching them who God says they are."

"Again, what does that even mean?"

"Well, like when they lie to you. You have to address the lying. But then you have to take some time to convince them that just because they can lie, it doesn't make them liars. That they have become something much more in Christ than just their behaviors. God hasn't changed His opinion of them because they lied, and you get to communicate that to them. Once they are convinced of this, it draws out who they really are. Does that make sense?"

"I think so. Maybe."

"All right. I need to slow down, don't I?"

Sarah replies, "Maybe. Yes."

"The moment we trust what Jesus did for us on the cross, we become new people. Really new! Not the same people as before just with a new coat of forgiveness paint. Follow me?"

"Yes. Maybe."

"Somehow, God's nature is joined with mine. I keep my same old tastes in wine and rock 'n' roll. But I'm changed, completely. As much changed as I'll ever be. I have this brand-new power to do right, to want to do right, instead of just doing right things."

"Okay, keep going. But go slowly."

"Sorry. I get a little excited." Allison chuckles.

"A little."

"So, let's pretend what I just said wasn't true. Let's say, in the case of parenting, they *didn't* have new power in them to want to do right, and that I couldn't appeal to that new nature. If that new power wasn't there, I'd have to exert my power to get them to obey, like by scolding them, berating them, or constantly nagging them. Right?"

"You just accurately described my parenting methodology."

"You and many others. But does nagging really work? Not really, does it? Kids don't really respond to such an approach or they respond superficially, for only a while. Eventually such parenting has diminishing returns. They either learn to comply to you and appease you to make things go smoothly or they learn to fight you."

"I've got one of each."

"But what if my premise was right? That, no matter how young or immature, the moment children come to Christ, they get a new heart. And that new heart, at its source, most wants to and actually has power to obey."

"Then, well, I guess I'd want to figure out how to tap into that new heart."

Allison cups both hands around her drink and brings it to her mouth. Before she takes a sip, she smiles and whispers, "Yes. Yes, you might."

"But I really don't know what I'd do differently. Are you saying all the rules and follow-up and trying to reiterate the instructions haven't been of any value?"

"It depends on what you're looking to accomplish. You can coerce and in the moment get them to comply with your wishes. You can make them feel guilty. You can exasperate them. You can pull rank. You can threaten them with loss of privileges. You can tell them till you're blue in the face, 'You should, you ought, what's wrong with you, why can't you, when will you?' But their hearts will remain unmoved. And whatever they do will be begrudgingly done, at the cost of feeling manipulated. And eventually, they will not trust you with their hearts."

"And now our strained relationship is added to the problem."

"Exactly. So, I began to ask this question: How do I encourage my kids to make good choices without unnecessarily making myself their issue?"

"I've done that too. Made myself their issue."

"They must be convinced that you know who they are. That

you never presume they are bent on always only wanting to get away with something. You must believe and convince them that you know at their core they want to obey God and you from the heart. You must draw out that response, even though it may not be their first response."

"Hmm. That's so good. I still don't know what that would look like. But I believe you."

"Even if children are not yet believers, you can still partially live with them this way. All of us, created in the image of God, are built to respond to grace. You can't yet appeal to their new identity, but you can treat them with dignity by not berating them or exasperating them. You can cause them to long for a new heart and help prepare them for that new heart. You won't go wrong treating your kids the way God treats you, even before they have placed faith in Him.

"Sarah, I love this saying: 'Grace as my motivation will always bear greater fruit than coercion or demand.'"

"This sounds hard to live out. Very hard."

"Yes. It's messy and exceedingly time consuming. But strained relationships between children and parents are even messier, more time consuming and less effective, satisfying, and enjoyable."

"I so want it to be enjoyable again."

"I did have to learn to care less about their appearance. Even their short-term behavioral inappropriateness. All so I could trust God's timing to mature them as they learned to trust God living through them. Then they could start to realize this was their relationship with God, not mine *for them*. They began, for the most part, to own their own faith.

"Gradually, my kids began to believe me. And, honey, their behaviors changed. As an added bonus, they knew my love. They could enjoy me. And I got to enjoy them. I could actually see it, feel it."

"As you're speaking, I'm remembering us all out to dinner recently with another family. Aiden said something that embarrassed me. It was nothing really. Just fifth-grade humor. He didn't even know he'd done anything wrong. But I didn't want to look foolish in front of this mom, whose kids always seem together and totally without issues."

"Don't you just hate them? Together-looking families?"

"Yes I do! I always want to yell out, 'Stop being so together! One of you, please, spill milk, belch, or talk back. Something. Anything! Don't you people ever do anything wrong? And why do all of you look like models for Patagonia?'"

"I know. I know."

"Anyway, I said something in front of everyone that made Aiden feel stupid. He was just being Aiden. But I was more concerned about what I looked like as a mother than about his feelings."

Allison nods, encouraging her to continue.

"The other night when Ray was lecturing Jim about Aiden's taste in clothes, I saw that look on Aiden's face. The same look as when I made him feel foolish in front of that family. It probably shamed him even more than Ray, coming from his own mom. I wish I could have a do-over on that evening."

"Yes. I've done all that and probably more."

"Allison, why haven't I heard this before?"

"Many of us were taught by well-intended teachers and parents that it almost doesn't matter what means you use to get someone to do good, as long as you can get them to do good. But good done for the wrong reason—convincing me that I, at my core, am not much good—that's one of the worst forms of wrong."

"My head is spinning."

"So maybe this will help. Andy was probably seventeen the day I walked into his room, looking for a matching sock. He'd left his computer on. I glanced over and suddenly pornography was staring at me. A partially naked woman. Enough to tell me my son had probably not stumbled onto it by accident. I froze. I didn't know what to do. I felt violated, lied to, embarrassed, angry. I felt like a failure. Like it was somehow my fault my son was looking at pornography. I thought I'd been doing everything the best I knew how. That I was showing them God in a right way.

"And now this. My son was drinking up pornography, apparently no different than a kid from a family of no faith. So, what was the God difference, after all? Suddenly I was a blur of severe, self-effort, religious fixes I thought I'd left behind years before. While I waited for him to return from basketball practice, I was rehearsing my responses: 'Andy, things are going to change now! You've taken advantage of me, taken advantage of God. This grace apparently doesn't work for you. How could you do this to us, to God? You're grounded from your computer, for, well, until I can figure out what to do next. Who did you get this from? How did you find this? Oh, and you can forget about going out with your friends tonight, and for a long time.'"

"I am so afraid of that day," Sarah responds. "I feel like it's probably already happening with Aiden."

"And then, in the next few minutes, God broke through. I started recalling the truths Helen Cacoris had been convincing me of:

> *The measurement of my faith convictions isn't about whether my kids keep from wrong behavior. The measurement is whether they're growing to depend upon God in the midst of their wrong behaviors.*

"I sat there wondering what I should say to Andy. Then I thought, almost out of nowhere, *Maybe I don't tell him anything. Maybe I give him a chance to tell me.*

"Sarah, if I'd owned it for Andy and laid down the law, it might have made me feel better. But I had to find a way to let the new life in him be revealed. He had to see God was powerful enough in him to handle his stuff.

"So, I thought, *Why not leave the screen up and wait?* I'd been telling my kids that God was continually wooing their hearts, encouraging them to let Him be stronger than their sin. I just needed to not get in the way of what I'd been telling them. I really had come to believe, *It's less important that anything gets fixed than that nothing has to be hidden.*

"But it scared me nearly to death to try it. Half an hour later Andy walked in. And nothing. He went to his room. Then he came down for dinner. Still nothing. He went to bed that evening without saying much of anything."

Sarah asks, "How did you keep from saying anything?"

"Oh, everything in me wanted to give the speech. But I had to believe God was working in Andy. And I couldn't change my approach now that my son had been revealed to actually be a real seventeen-year-old, exposed to what he would have eventually seen no matter how I parented him. The real question was: Now that it's revealed, am I a safe enough place to give him a way home?

"Several days went by. That next Saturday, the two of us were out back, turning over soil from the summer garden.

"He said, 'Mom, may I tell you something? Do you promise to not freak out?'

"'No, I don't. But go ahead.'

"'The last few weeks I've been looking at...'

"I decided to not say anything. I just kept turning over soil.

"Andy went on. 'At pictures of women on the computer.'

"'I know.'

"'What? You know what?'

"'About the pictures.'

"He asked, 'How?'

"I answered, 'I'm a mom. I'm paid to know.'

"He asked me what I wanted to do.

"I found myself saying, 'I think we're doing it. Andy, you just told on yourself.'

"'I did, didn't I?'

"He told me that he had tried to get away with it for several weeks. I thanked him for telling me. And I reminded him that he had a new heart and hiding would never ultimately be easy anymore.

"He told me that hiding was killing him.

"I asked, 'So, what should I have done if you didn't tell me?'

"'I guess you would have eventually had to tell me you knew.'

"'And then what?'

"He thought for a while. 'And then we would have faced it together.' He looked at me and smiled. 'Like we pretty much do everything. Mom, I wasn't really afraid to tell you. I was embarrassed. But I knew you wouldn't see me differently. Most of my friends would never tell their moms this stuff.'

"'So, what do we do now?' I asked him.

"'I don't know,' he answered. 'Could I maybe start telling you when this stuff comes up?'

"So, Sarah, there's that. Is any of this making sense?"

"Yes. Maybe more than you can know. I really think I'm hearing you, Allison."

"Thank you. I've waited a long time to wander into this talk. Thanks for listening to an old woman ramble. Maybe that's enough for now. Do you like your tea?"

"I love it. I'm ruined for Lipton. I'll have to get one of these strainers."

"Your birthday is coming up soon. We'll get you started out right."

"Thank you, Allison. I feel like I'm having one of those moments I won't soon forget. Do you know what I mean?"

"Yes, I do, dear. Me too."

WHEN YOU BUILD ME UP

The next morning there are tearful goodbyes. Allison presents Sarah with a teapot, a strainer, and all manner of tea-making accoutrements. Aiden gets a Bob Dylan album.

And the Clawsons are back in the car.

Madison speaks for the entire family, looking back at Allison waving. "I want to grow up to be like Grandma."

Today they will wind their way through Yosemite National Park. Before leaving the park they stop for a hike and snacks, looking up at some of the great landmarks of the park: El Capitan, Yosemite Falls, and Half Dome.

Then they are out of the park by late mid-afternoon. They have a time-share reservation in Mammoth Lakes for this evening and the next.

As they leave Yosemite and begin their drive down California 395, they play a portion of the "Enjoy the Ride."

Once again, on comes the soothing-voiced woman who has become their guide. A friend. They each hold her responsible for some pain, much goodness, and so much new hope.

Several sentences in, Aiden interrupts: "I think this lady and Grandma would be friends."

"There are few things we get to do on this planet with more value than affirming another. It causes other people's faith to grow as they watch what they have asked God to do in them, being expressed by someone whose affirmation they trust."

By late afternoon they've driven eighty miles south to Mammoth Lakes. Friends back in Phoenix own a great time-share there and have encouraged the Clawsons to use it for as long as they like on their way back home.

As the sun begins to set on this day, the four are seated on padded Adirondack chairs on a second-floor deck, overlooking a cobblestoned lane of shops, pubs, and restaurants. Jim earlier declared this evening to be "The Clawsons' Vacation Junk Food Fest." Their hastily assembled menu has lived up to the billing. On the patio table are two large cheese pizzas and two orders of spicy hot wings, next to industrial-sized bags of Cheetos and salt and vinegar chips. A one-pound package of peanut M&M's is propped up against an oily paper bag filled with tacos, taquitos, sour cream, guacamole, and salsa. The cooler contains sizable containers of Ben and Jerry's ice cream and six-packs of cream soda and root beer. There's even a quart bottle of Diet Squirt. Why not?

They ordered a salad with the pizza, but even it is slathered in blue cheese dressing with bacon crumbles. You have to search hard to find anything healthy in this array.

Jim plays one of his playlists from his phone, so Pearl Jam and U2 get an inordinate amount of playtime over the next forty-five minutes.

Everyone is stuffed and comfortably reclined when Sarah passes out a handful of pens and lays a stack of paper on the table.

"Okay, affirmation. I thought it would be great if we tried it out with each other."

Ten days ago this activity would have been shot down, met with mutinous groans and apathetic disdain. Sarah would have pulled back and reminded herself that she was a lousy parent who should never try to initiate anything of spiritual value.

But not tonight.

Everyone grabs paper.

"So, across the page, write the names of each of the other three. Below each name, think of three positive things you really like about them. Not necessarily what they do best but who they are. Pick three. Like 'thoughtful' or 'caring' or 'funny.' Then, think about what you'd want to tell that person to explain why you picked that description.

"Oh, yes. The person being affirmed can't say anything until the one affirming is completely done. Then you get to say how the affirmation made you feel, if you'd like. Does that all make sense?"

There are no questions. Everyone starts writing.

At first there is some nervous awkwardness. Madison asks, "May we use profanity?"

They all laugh, hard.

Then it gets quiet. Very quiet. Everyone is scouring their memories.

After a long silence Sarah calls out, "So, let's pick our first person, in no particular order. Who wants to go?"

The Clawsons have never done anything like this.

Aiden asks, "I want to go. May I go first?"

"Yes. Of course, Aiden. Are you sure?"

"I'm sure."

Aiden stands up. He looks around at everyone, then fully at Jim.

"Dad, my word for you is 'brave.' I think brave is when you do something even though you're scared. That night in Monterey, when you told Madison that you hurt her feelings? That was brave. I was mad at you, too. And then you did that. So, thanks."

Everyone is staring at Jim now, smiling at him. He smiles at Aiden for a moment. Then he looks away. This is a strange new country for him. He isn't sure what to do. He grabs a handful of M&M's. No words are spoken.

Just when it seems like the moment has passed, Aiden blurts out, "Oh, and that day when you didn't yell at me for forgetting my hat down at the beach. I don't know what to call that. You had us all go back together to get it. We were together, that felt really good. So that."

Sarah speaks up. "Thank you, Aiden. Great job."

Madison playfully shoves Aiden with a thumbs-up.

"So," Sarah asks Jim. "How did that make you feel?"

Jim looks up and takes in a deep breath. He leans forward, looking directly into Aiden's eyes.

"Aiden, thank you. After the way this trip got started, I really wouldn't have thought my name would even come up on this exercise. So thank you."

He looks each of his family members in the eyes. He shakes his head, involuntarily smiling, and grabs another handful of M&M's.

"My turn now!" Sarah calls out.

She looks at Madison and says quietly, as if only for her hearing, "Are you ready for this?"

Madison nods.

"Madison, I wrote this down for you: 'truth-teller.' You were so miserable as we started this trip. You were hurt and angry. You had every right to be. But in less than two weeks, you have become a fan of our family. And in the process you have shared truth with each of us at different times on this vacation. Madison, I'm learning to trust your words, both in the statements you make and the questions you ask. I'm sorry I didn't do this before." Sarah leans forward. "You're amazing."

Tears are filling Sarah's eyes. "I love you, Madison."

"I love you too, Mom."

They are sitting next to each other. Madison leans over and puts her head on her mom's shoulder.

After a few moments, Madison straightens up and says, "So. Do I get to tell how what you said made me feel?"

Sarah nods, smiling, as yet unable to speak.

"That felt good. I didn't feel like our family was close at all, and that you never listened to me. Now, you call me a 'truth-teller.' Even though I don't always show it, I love all of you. Mom, thanks."

"You're so welcome."

Jim blurts out, "Okay, I didn't write any of this on my paper. But I have to say this. Sarah, thank you. This whole thing we're doing here. You risked this. You sometimes don't think you were cut out for being a mom. But you're a great mom, and a great wife. And this last week and a half, I've gotten to see that we're really a pretty great family. Sorry if I went out of turn."

"Oh." Jim picks up his paper and reads from it. "And I did write down a phrase. The one I picked for your mom was 'smoking hot!'"

The other three erupt with shocked laughter and groans. In decades to come, this moment will grow into an often-told anecdote Madison and Aiden will recount to their children and grandchildren at holiday dinners and family gatherings.

Aiden says, "And Grandpa thinks *I* do weird stuff."

More laughter. Just that Aiden could say those words—"Grandpa thinks *I* do weird stuff," that he could put that embarrassing moment on the table and laugh about it—shows his family's affirmation is stronger than his grandpa's hurtful words. They all four know this is a redemptive moment.

This exercise goes long into the evening as each is affirmed by the others. Eventually, everyone stops reading their written affirmations, as story after story continues to pour out.

This evening was designed by a mom beginning to believe she is God's exact choice to parent her kids. And it was wonderfully allowed by a father, beginning to figure out how to be fully in the moment with his family.

INSIDE THE EPISODE

Proverbs 27:2 teaches, "Let another praise you, and not your own mouth."

For so long, especially in our faith communities, we have been told to be sparing with affirmation—for fear our egos will grow, our heads will get bigger, and we will become arrogant and narcissistic.

In truth, it is affirmation's absence that has caused so much of our bragging and manipulative attempts to get others to tell us we're worth knowing and loving.

Far from puffing us up, honest affirmation humbles us. It causes us to want to do more of what we're being affirmed for in the family or community or organization blessing us.

Affirmation heals. It dispels sarcasm and cynicism. It actually protects us from self-protection. It gives us confidence, boldness, creativity, and freedom. It teaches how to actively love.

We get to communicate God's specific expressions of delight to each other. Anytime it is done in truth and authenticity, we are experiencing love words from God to a human, prepared from before the world began!

The Father affirmed the Son, the Son affirmed the Father, and the apostle Paul affirmed Timothy. Affirmation can transform relationships between a husband and wife, in a business, in a church, and in a family on birthdays, or at any milestone, including the beginning of a new chapter of life.

E PISODE
NINE

IN THE RING WITH THE
BULLS OF REALITY

The Clawsons' first order of business the next morning is to find a car wash. They purchase the top-of-the-line, automated "Deluxe Wash" that includes a much-needed hanging air freshener. Aiden and Madison vacuum up the last ten days of the road, while Jim and Sarah toss accumulated wrappers, magazines, receipts, park passes, and soda cans.

They then stop at Schat's Bakery, where they order sandwiches and pastries for a day trip out to Convict Lake, ten miles south of town.

Almost instinctually now, Sarah turns on the podcast. There is time for at least part of one.

"So how do parents teach their children how to make healthy decisions? It is never passed on without intention. But many of us have never really thought through how and why we have made the decisions we

chose. We're unequipped to guide our kids into a process of healthy decisions we have never learned ourselves.

"We can be unwilling to let our kids know about the failures in our past because we are afraid our vulnerability will give them the wrong kind of permission. But in doing this, we remain unknown to our children.

"When we remain unknown, we leave them alone in their decision making and they become vulnerable to repeating the same wrong choices we made.

"As a bad substitute, many of us replace relational vulnerability with impersonal behavioral technique, hoping it will do the job. But our kids smell it. They know they are being managed, not parented.

"Without the gift of our vulnerability, they are forced to learn to make decisions on their own. But they don't have the maturity to understand a basis for their choices. Then when they do choose poorly, parents often dole out punishment for their wrong choices. It is a vicious cycle. No direction to help them into right choices and punishment for the inevitable wrong choices.

"But wait! There is a way off this tilt-a-whirl. This script can be wonderfully and vitally rewritten in this generation.

"The issues affecting the process of our decision making are rooted in our motives and values. A motive is our basic drive or goal in life.

"Our motives establish our values. Then all of our actions come out of those values.

"So as parents, we want to help our kids find their way back to the starting place of motive. Because motive reveals the deep, honest attitude of our hearts. We want to help our children get in touch with the honest attitude of their hearts, which ultimately releases the behaviors.

"When you tell your life story or pieces of it to your kids, you teach your evaluation of the consequences of your choices. Instead *of them only vaguely knowing their parents did this or that back sometime in the past, you get to be the one who tells them what really happened and how it affected you and those around you. You get to protect them by giving them an example of what they're facing now, but with your evaluation of the consequences. So you are letting them see your heart's motivation for why you did what you did. This allows them a window into their own motivations.*

"This is one of the greatest influences we can have as parents."

They shut off the podcast just as Convict Lake opens up in front of them. Jim finds a parking spot directly across from the lake.

The lake got its name from an incident on September 23, 1871. Convicts who escaped from a Carson City prison were trapped and met their end at the unscalable mountain face on the far end of the lake. The name doesn't do this place any justice. A three-mile walk takes hikers around a neon-blue picture postcard of water, with dramatic cliffs surrounding it. Close nearby there are pine cabins, picnic tables, a restaurant, general store and fishing boat rental slips. It's a magnificent destination for a final day before the Clawsons make their last push across the desert for home.

Aiden jumps out of the car, runs to the other side of the road and yells back, "Whoa! Look at the color of that water! Mom, Dad! Can we go out on a boat?"

"Well, I don't know. Jim, what do you think?"

"Madison," Jim asks. "What would you like to do?"

"I kinda just wanted to hike."

"Me too. Do you mind if I go with you?"

"Not as long as you carry the backpack with the sandwiches."

"Deal. Sarah, why don't you and Aiden go out on a boat?"

"Can we really, Mom?" Aiden asks.

Sarah smiles and says, "Well, I've never really driven a boat."

Madison laughs, "They're aluminum. How much damage can you do?"

"You forget about the bus."

"Bus?" Jim asks.

Madison smiles. "Nothing. Um, just, you know, a bus." She looks back at Sarah. "You'll be fine, Mom."

There's a glance and a moment's pause from Jim, then a head shake and a move back to what he was doing.

They all apply sunscreen, not wanting another episode like Morro Beach, and divide up their picnic food.

And just like that, the family breaks into pairs. Jim and Madison walk the circumference of Convict Lake while Sarah and Aiden rent a boat with a trolling motor.

Twenty minutes into their hike, Jim and Madison glance back and notice Sarah and Aiden are on the lake, but flailing to maneuver out of the boat dock area. Nearly across the lake, they can hear Sarah and Aiden half laughing, half panicking as they dodge the other boats tied up along either side of the entrance onto the lake.

Sometimes the finest things to be said about family members come when you're watching them from a distance.

"It's cool Mom would do that with Aiden." Madison laughs. "Wow! Mom driving a boat."

They watch the boat slowly flounder toward an opening, seemingly adrift.

Jim adds, "Aiden is probably starting to reconsider his decision about now."

Jim and Madison both sit under the shade of pine trees, looking out at the beautiful landscape and their hapless family members.

"It occurred to me, listening to the podcast this morning..."

"I know what you're going to say. And, Dad, you don't have to."

"How do you know what I'm going to say?"

"I watched you look back at me in the mirror when the lady was talking about how parents leave their kids alone to figure out decisions. How parents need to learn to tell more of their stories to their kids."

"Too obvious, huh?"

"A little."

"Well, what do you want to know? What dark secrets of my past do you want to hear?"

"Seriously? Here? Now?"

Jim points across the lake to Sarah and Aiden's boat. They're finally puttering along a semi-intentional path across the lake. "I think we've got some time. Your mom's getting the hang of things. But they could be out there awhile."

"No, Dad. You tell me. What should I know?"

"Nice move, Madison. Fair enough." He thinks for a moment, stands up, and brushes pine needles off his legs as a signal that it's time to hike.

"I stole my best friend's girlfriend away from him. While they were engaged. Maybe you should know that."

"Dad! What?"

"Just before I met your mom."

"Oh my gosh! Why?"

"See, that's the thing. I still don't know. It kind of haunts me. Because I've done other things like that too. I just did it. Impulse is the best word I have for it. She was beautiful and cool and funny. And I wanted to be with her. It sounds really wrong now. But it made all the sense in the world at the time."

They're walking single file, Jim leading the way on the narrow path above the circumference of the lake.

"But what about your best friend?"

"Sean Cavanaugh. He and I were roommates at ASU." He stops and turns to face Madison. "Why am I even telling you this?"

"Keep going."

"All right. But you're going to lose some respect for me."

"Dad, this is the first time in my whole life you've ever told me anything bad about you. How did you break them up?"

The gears in Jim's head are moving at the speed of hummingbird wings.

"He went home for Christmas for a week, and I just started showing up at her apartment more and more. I knew I was going to try to move in on her weeks before."

They start walking again.

"Madison, I just wish I would have known."

"Known what?"

"I wish I'd known that it would hurt people down the line because I gave myself permission to do whatever I wanted without caring about what it would do to them."

"What does that mean?"

"I want you to learn stuff from me. But I'm not a very good example. See, early on I learned how to take care of me, just me. How to make things go my way. How to manipulate it so I won."

"Weren't you a Christian by then?"

"Yes, I was. I think decisions like taking Sean's girlfriend kind of started me on a path that has messed up my thinking. There are times when I think there's something really wrong with me that can't be changed, even by God. That even though I'm a Christian, I'll still just do what works for me. Even when it hurts your mother, or anyone else, in the process. Even you, Madison. I hate that."

Madison is soaking this up like a sponge. She's never had a conversation like this with her dad. Her circuits are flooding with hope as they silently walk the next half mile.

The path winds down closer to the water at the far end of the lake, revealing several picnic tables. Madison pulls out a bear-claw pastry and breaks it in half, handing one part to her dad as they sit down.

"So, am I just going to make the same bad choices? I'm pretty sure I already am."

"Madison, I don't exactly know. I was thinking that same thing this morning. I so don't want you to make those same mistakes. I think it must have something to do with why I come down so hard on you sometimes."

"Podcast lady was talking about motives. What was your motive when you stole your best friend's girlfriend?"

More laughter and chaos drift across the lake from the boat. It appears Aiden's hat has gone in the water. And he has gone in after it, nearly taking Sarah into the lake with him.

"Madison, you're asking a hard question. And I hate the answer."

"Keep going, Dad."

"I think I wanted him to know I was a better man than he was. That I was capable of taking his girlfriend if I wanted to. Ugh. How's that for a screwed-up motive?"

Madison is ready to respond, but Jim discovers he is not done.

"So, I guess I need to say this. Because I don't know if I'll ever think it like this again. I'd better say it while it's here."

"What?"

"I think I have been living with the consequences of what I did to Sean ever since then. This is hard. Give me a moment."

He stands up like he is going to start walking again, but only turns a full circle and sits back down.

"After that experience, I learned not to trust myself. Madison, that's still true. I'm embarrassed at what I'm saying. But its probably even affecting my parenting you. I don't trust my motives for why I'm parenting you the way I am. I actually sometimes think that I don't even have the right to parent you. So instead of talking about something that matters, instead of being vulnerable with you, I just power up and try to be the better man again. Does that make any sense?"

"Yeah. That is really screwed up, Dad." She gives him a half-smile.

"Yep."

"But I get it. I've already done some stuff like that with my friends. But not that bad!"

She gives him the other half of that smile.

He speaks as though to the lake. "Podcast lady is messing me up."

"Have you ever talked to him about that?"

"Who?"

"Sean."

"No. I don't even know where he is these days. How sad is that?"

It's quiet between them for a minute. Both are working hard with what has just been talked about.

"So what's changed?"

"What do you mean, Madison?"

"You look back and hate what you did. So what's changed?"

"You mean like my motive?"

"Yeah, I guess."

"I guess, over time, believing in Jesus, I've realized I want to love people more than I want to just win. That somehow loving people is the way to being the better man. But I've lived that other way for a long time, so it's kind of wet cement. About the time I think I'm making progress, I screw things up."

"Thanks, Dad."

Jim and Madison sit at the water's edge in silence. Sometimes silence is golden.

They're six hundred miles from home, but Jim and Madison are as at home with each other as they've ever been.

INSIDE THE EPISODE

"Consequential decision making." True, that's probably not a phrase you've heard recently (or ever) in the checkout lane at the grocery store. But we all know what it means: Every decision is attached to a consequence. No decision happens in a vacuum. And the consequence of a decision will always affect you and someone other than you. Maybe a lot more people than you.

Circumstances present themselves each day. In all circumstances there are opportunities. But not all opportunities come from God. If all one needs to miss the purposes of God is to be seduced by opportunity, then all darkness will encourage you to take the bait. Opportunity does not guarantee it is coupled with integrity, faithfulness, or the intention of God. Immature decision makers may want what appears to give reward, status, and meaning, even if it costs integrity.

So in all circumstances, I have to determine: "What do I truly want?" What I really "want" is my motive. My motive leads to motion, to action. Sitting with Madison at the lake, Jim was getting in touch with the motive that allowed him to steal his best friend's girlfriend. He wanted to prove he was the "better man." He would prove he was more of a man by taking another man's relationship. If Jim's motive had been to love his best friend, he would have honored his friend's relationship.

Jim stumbling with Madison through his own story ultimately helped her discover and get in touch with her own motives for the things she is doing.

It's an astonishing gift to your children for you to begin to determine what your convictions are. Parents have the magnificent privilege of helping their children ask the why questions. It is exponentially different than asking, "What did you do?" The better question is, "Why do you think you did it?" That is a motive question. Asking why questions shifts the balance of the world toward goodness. But unless we are willing to answer the question in our own lives, we will never earn the right to ask it in anybody else's.

Our model in this is Jesus. He trusted God with Himself so He could serve us. He did everything He could for our benefit. That's our wonderful model for those of us who have placed our hope in Him.

The process of consequential decision making creates avoidance in immature parents. The immature most often see themselves as victims of their choices rather than responsible for their choices. When parents avoid their own personal development, they're less able to teach their children the process of consequential decision making. Instead of becoming engaged protectors, they become managers, less able to guide their children into their futures.

Do not be afraid to let your children in on the stories of your bad choices. As you share your life story—the good and the bad and the ugly—you get to teach them your evaluation of the consequences of your choices. In the process, you protect them by letting them learn what really happened and why. From your honest expression of the events and consequences of your choice, they're free to see a new path forward, freed from repeating what harmed you.

This is a great exercise to go through with your child:

Parent to child (in other words, parents go first):
♦   Explain a time you made a bad decision.
♦   Why do you think you made that decision?
♦   How did you know it was a bad decision?
♦   How did you deal with the consequences of the bad decision?

Child to parent (in other words, child answers):
♦   When was the last time you made a bad decision?
♦   Why do you think you made that decision?
♦   How did you know it was a bad decision?
♦   Have you resolved the bad decision?
♦   How have you reacted when your parent expressed a wrong decision they made?

This exchange will take time. And stories of our life experience must be told differently to different ages. Not all kids are initially excited to hear of their parent's failures when such vulnerability has been absent for so long. They may want to know why this has been withheld from them. But all sons and daughters, the older they get, long to hear their parents telling the truth about themselves. They are waiting for their parents' interpretation of the consequences. For they innately know they are approaching the same decisions. And they need to think through establishing God-centered motives that create life-giving values, which issue in life-freeing behavior.

This is a huge opportunity for a parent to trust what God is doing and avoid trite, manipulative, superspiritual-sounding answers. For example, "And then your father saw the error of his ways. And that is the day he stopped smoking. And he gave all that money he was spending on cigarettes to an orphanage in Bogotá. And God has blessed him financially for it. And that's how your mom and dad have come to have a nice boat. This is why you should obey your father and mother in everything they say or do."

Just don't do that. Ever.

Or, "In high school, even though everyone else was going out on the weekends and doing wrong, I did not. I obeyed God and my parents, so I stayed home and read the Bible. Often, in those evenings, I wrote letters to shut-ins and ironed my own clothes. I can't remember a time when I disobeyed my parents. Except maybe when I kept writing letters to shut-ins after I was supposed to turn out the lights for bed."

We're exaggerating a little in these two examples, but only a little. We've heard such examples, almost verbatim, drop from parents' lips.

Parents who can only tell their story through the glorified lens of spiritual sacrifice and superior commitment to God end up with children feeling only shame and failure when they can't respond to life with such ironclad victory. And then later, when they discover their parents didn't really face life with such overly heroic faith, it's too late. The child feels lost, with no clue as to how to navigate real life. They desperately need to hear the stories of what God has done and what still is remaining to be done. This is the gift of authentic faith. God always loves a good story. And a good story means all of it.

BACK TO EPISODE 9: IN THE RING WITH THE BULLS OF REALITY

Meanwhile, Aiden is back in the aluminum boat, reunited with his hat, breathlessly rehearsing the adventure with his mom in the middle of Convict Lake.

Sarah is staring at her sopping-wet son. She is suddenly caught off guard with a sensation she has not felt for as long as she can remember. Her cheeks are hurting from laughing.

Less than two weeks ago, Sarah sat on the sand at Newport Beach, also staring at her son. She was filled with regret and shame at not knowing how to love her kids well, convicted of throwing around edicts like her mom instead of calling out the best in them.

In the last hour, the place in the universe Sarah most wishes to be is *right here.* And the person she wants most to be with is sitting *right across from her.* And this is exactly what she wants to be doing.

It's a stunning God moment when you discover you are not who you feared you were. Instead, you are who you feared you might never be—a real, honest, unfeigned lover. All it takes for this moment to happen is to believe that God has made it so.

Later that evening, the Clawsons are back at the condo, packing for an early start back to Phoenix. So much good has happened in these last dozen days. They are each spending their last evening enjoying the freedom of doing their own thing.

When God intervenes in a family in such a miraculous way, it is not unlike anesthesia after surgery. There is a wonderful, drugged comfort, lulling people into believing everything will be pain-free for the rest of their lives.

Until the anesthesia wears off.

After today's miracles merge with tomorrow's reality, they awaken to discover they still carry patterns, histories, default systems, and wounds. And they don't go away quietly with good teaching or even remarkable God moments.

It starts with an innocent remark. Both Jim and Sarah are packing, and Jim makes a playful statement still stunned with excitement from his conversation with Madison earlier in the day.

"I wish you could have listened in on our talk today."

Then, a careless response, born of Sarah's knee-jerk mistrust of Jim's interactions with Madison.

"Are you sure she felt the same way?"

"What?"

"Nothing."

"Sarah, what did that mean?"

"You know what it meant."

"No, I don't. What was that supposed to mean? *'Are you sure she felt that way?'* Why did you say that?"

"Jim, I'm sure it was fine."

Jim waits until Sarah makes eye contact.

"I never do it right, do I? And you're always more than happy to point that out with those little jabs."

"Jim, stop it. I don't want to do this. We've had a good day. We've had a really good trip."

"And?"

"And, I don't want to fight with you. Just drop it. I'm sorry I said it. I'm sure you had a good talk with Madison."

But it's too late. The wire has been tripped. Jim takes the bait.

Just like in Newport Beach and so many dozens of times before that. Nothing they've known so far has been enough to allow their faith to break this sinister code and stop the relational madness. In the old way of relating, there's no way out of this kind of interaction until the poison gets fully spent.

"A good trip, but nothing's changed, has it, Sarah? It's still the same. You're the good parent. I'm a monster. God, I hate this."

"Jim, we've talked about this a hundred times. You get rough on people. Like your kids. Like you're doing to me, right now. You feel disrespected. But it's not about us. It's about you, Jim."

Loudly, Jim says, "That's not true."

"And here we go. You get loud and you win. And we all lose."

That. Right there. That knife of a line. That stabbing in of her version of his failure. With uninterruptable quickness and repetition, she's skilled at this.

And in the time it takes to breathe, all objectivity on Jim's part dissolves. He says words he will not be able to retrieve.

"Are you freakin' kidding me? *'We all lose'?* Oh wow, I've never heard that line before, Sarah. That's so original. Thank you so much for your enlightened bullshit. What would I do without you? Oh, I know, maybe have a chance at feeling loved. God, I honestly think you enjoy sticking the knife in and turning the blade."

She is stunned.

They both are.

It is not the first time she has heard words like these. But in light of the last twelve days, this time feels especially dark.

"I don't like you, Sarah."

"Message received, Jim, loud and clear. Oh, just don't forget, no one in this family trusts you. Okay?"

They are standing across the bed, now turned away from each other. She is still holding several pairs of folded shorts in her arms, as though they represent the only remaining control in her world.

Quick, loud, irrational snippets of how she will get out of this run drunk through her mind: *I will be quiet until we get home. Then, on Monday I will call a divorce counselor. I'll talk to the kids. No, Jim can talk to the kids. He can explain what he did to cause this. But I do want out. I will not be the victim of this control any longer.*

Jim is fuming. After her meanness he feels totally vindicated in what he said. He thinks, *I've been trying to do everything she wanted me to do. But like always, it's never enough.*

Both are settled in for no resolution. Jim is considering where he'll sleep tonight in this crowded condo. Certainly not in bed with Sarah.

Then, in the time it takes to breathe, it happens. God intervenes.

Jim discovers a previously unresourced place to reach in and pull out something stronger.

It is nearly involuntary. But it's the direct fruit of a growing trust of God, rekindled in Jim on this trip.

In a series of quick snapshots, he first sees a replay of the moment back in Sausalito when he protected Aiden against the unkindness of his own father. Then his walk with Madison on the trail behind Allison's home, where he chose to stop powering up and admit he doesn't know what to say or do. He sees Allison looking into his eyes as he describes her impact on his faith. He sees Madison saying "thank you" to him, on the far end of Convict Lake.

Convictions attaching themselves to motives are now forming at the core of his heart.

These words from Galatians 2:20 find him and pour all over him: *"I have been crucified with Christ; and it is no longer I who live, but Christ lives in me; and the life which I now live in the flesh I live by faith in the Son of God, who loved me and gave Himself up for me."*

Then these thoughts: *I don't have to always go to this. I'm Christ in Jim Clawson. I can love, right now. Do it, Jim. Do it. Say her name.*

Jim turns around. He quietly calls out, "Sarah." He waits until she turns around, which is not immediately.

"Sarah, I'm so sorry. What I just said, it's so wrong. That's not what I want. It's not who I am. I love you, Sarah. You may not believe that right now. But I do believe you love me. You're right. I power up. I scare you. This is about me. God, please help me trust Your power to stop hurting Sarah like this. Please help me. I want to believe I am who You say I am. And I want it to be more than words. I'm so sorry."

Sarah has been here before. She has heard well-crafted apologies from Jim. They come when he realizes he has stepped too far. And he has stepped too far. She is way past angry. She is calculated and resolved. Still, something is different right now—something in the way he said what he just said. She just needs to stop long enough to sort through what is happening. She is about to respond when she hears Madison.

"Mom? Dad?"

The bedroom door, which Jim thought he closed at the start of the argument, now stands wide open. In the doorway stand Madison and Aiden.

Madison says, "We heard everything. Everything."

The Clawsons are on the verge of big choices. Everything changes from here. All four have the same skin in this game now. All four must own their part in the journey.

For most families in a situation like this, children rightfully withdraw into their own pain and pretend these last ten minutes never happened. They would have never opened the door and would have never admitted they heard the fight. They would stuff their fear and their own shame. They would both live even more convinced that their parents cannot handle them. From this time on, they would go it alone.

For most families in a situation like this, the parents would try to minimize the severity of what was overheard. They would enact a version of "kiss and make up" in front of the kids. But no one would believe it, and the children would trust their parents less for being willing to hide reality from them.

But today, light has entered. Humility and trust in the power and character of God have been discovered. The seeds of redemption and vulnerable honesty have been planted. And the freedom to love is growing.

What happens next will be awkward like this family has never experienced before. But it will also be astonishingly supernatural. Nothing between Jim and Sarah has been resolved. But this is very different from the cover-up in Newport Beach. This is not denial. This is a family in the ring with the bulls of reality.

Aiden and then Madison slowly move toward the bed and climb onto it. Jim and Sarah join their children, sitting on either side.

"I'm so sorry you both had to hear that," Sarah says.

After a moment, Aiden speaks first. "Dad, you scared me."

Before Jim can respond, Madison says, "I've never, ever heard you two do that."

"You've never heard us fight?"

"Not like that. Not like for real."

As she says these words, Madison begins to cry.

In many families, *a messy but beautifully relational life has been replaced by a sanitized and technique-driven one.*

In this moment, we are watching the polar opposite take place. The sanitized, technique-driven life is being replaced with the messy but exquisitely relational one.

It started some days ago as a cautious and barely understood experiment of trust by two parents. *"Because God's primary goal is earning my trust and to increasingly mature me, correct my behavior, and free my life, I will attempt to offer the same for my child."*

The Clawsons sit on the bed together, well into the night. They shift positions, move to chairs, or pace while others are talking. The kids ask hard questions:

"Do you love Mom?"

"Mom, why are you so mean to Dad?"

"Are you two going to get a divorce?"

"Dad, did you swear at Mom?"

"Have you had a lot of fights like this?"

Jim and Sarah try to answer with hard, age-appropriate, but accurate and compassionate answers. Both of them take time to answer everything and then ask if they did answer their questions.

Then, in front of Madison and Aiden, Jim and Sarah take a stab at a rough form of repentance and forgiveness for what was said.

For now it is enough that Jim says, "I don't know how to do this right. But, Sarah, I'm sorry I hurt you. Would you please tell me what I did? I want to own all of it. Please don't hold back."

Sarah does not hold back. She pours out her sadness, not only from this fight, but from Jim's historic control and unwillingness to ever stand down. She says it with a bravery and honesty, as if the kids are not even there.

But then she says, "As I sat here, listening, I realize, Jim, that I have not forgiven you. And it has been making me unhealthy. I've accused you of things you do not deserve. I give you little credit when you do love well. I've pulled away from you. I'm so, so sorry. I don't know if you'll ever change. But I know I am not to be your judge and jury. God does that. He must be the one who protects me in the meantime.

"So a few minutes ago, while you were talking to the kids, I decided to forgive you. I'm done being your cop. God can do the protecting and convicting. I'm done being sick. And I swear, although I may regret saying this… I'm choosing to love you, Jim."

Jim slowly walks around the bed to where Sarah is sitting. She stands and he holds her. And he begins to cry.

Jim rarely cries. Jim especially does not cry in front of his kids. Jim has never cried with his family sitting on a bed.

But tonight Jim can cry. Between sobs, tissues, gulps, and words that take so long to come, he stammers, "I'm sorry, to you all. I've been trying to hold us together with, I don't know, my power and rightness. I didn't let you know me, I made you resent and rebel against rules and control. I'm sorry for how much I've hurt each of you. I only know how wrong I've been. But I know so little yet of how to do it differently.

"Sarah, you have never deserved my devaluing you. You are a beautiful woman, mom, and wife. I can't take back tonight's words. But I want to earn new ones. I'm listening. Teach me how to love you well. I love you so. I'm sorry that I have made you feel less than or stupid or weak."

He tries for more words, but they do not come.

Sarah waits for a moment before she speaks. Then, she says words that surprise everyone in the room, maybe most of all her. "No, Jim. This can't end like it always does. Those words you spoke were wrong. They hurt me, and they will not easily go away. But…" She sighs and turns away, then back again. "Jim, this was as much me as it was you. I push and bait and goad until you say the thing that makes you the bad guy. That's what I do, and I've gotten really good at it. I've fought that way for as long as I can remember. Kids, you've seen me do it. I win, but the fight's not fair. Jim, I decided a minute ago to forgive you. Can you please forgive me? I'm really sorry. Oh God, I'm sorry. I've never admitted any of this before. Jim, please forgive me."

Now she too is crying.

No more is said, by anyone. The entire family knows they've worked through more tonight than any of them ever imagined before this trip began. They hug each other and the kids quietly leave the room.

Earlier on the trip, the woman on the podcast shared this:

"'Put on the new self, which in the likeness of God has been created in righteousness and holiness of the truth' (Ephesians 4:24, NASB). If we can trust the truth in this, it will radically alter everything that comes next.

"This changes our entire way of parenting. This changes how we believe God sees us. This changes how we see ourselves. This changes how we see our children. This changes how they can see themselves.

"Putting on the new self allows us to see ourselves, and our children, as saints and not saved sinners. Plus, it allows us to appeal to Christ in us to parent well, and to begin learning how to appeal to the new nature in our children. And if our children are not yet believers, it models a God-trusting life so our children will recognize authentic faith when the time comes."

On this night, the Clawsons tried on their new selves. They've each possessed this new self from the moment they placed their hope in Jesus. But this family now has a new default. This family has seen a new way of living. This family has experienced the power of God showing up. They have experienced that, on their worst day, they are indeed holy and righteous, fused with Jesus, able to love sacrificially. This family's generational patterns have been radically altered.

This family is learning to trust.

*E*PISODE
TEN

SOMEONE TO WATCH
OVER ME

Y ou're probably wishing you could be a fly on the wall some
months after that last episode ended. Well, as you wish.

Seven Months Later:

It is 6:08 p.m. Jim knows the exact time, because he's been
checking his phone every minute or so the last twenty minutes.
Madison was supposed to be home over an hour ago. She has not
been answering her phone. Sarah has stopped reheating her dinner.
Sarah has called several of Madison's closest friends and nobody
seems to know where she is. Aiden is over at a friend's house before
they go to youth group at church. She has called over there to see if
he has heard anything. So far, nothing.

Jim has gone from care to concern to frustration to feeling
disrespected to fear. He has now moved to angry, disrespected fear.

"She knows to call if she's going to be late. If we've made
anything clear, it's that."

"Jim, we don't know what's going on. She'll be home. She may have just lost track of time. Maybe she lost her phone or something."

"That would make sense if she was the only one in Phoenix with a phone. Unless she's being held by terrorists, she could use someone else's phone to call us."

"Don't, Jim."

"Don't what?" Then louder. "Don't *what?*" Jim's looking for a fight. But the person he wants to fight with is an hour and ten minutes late for dinner.

"You're doing it again."

"Doing what again? Caring about my daughter?"

"We all care about her. Not just you."

Jim looks again at his watch: 6:12.

To complicate matters, Jeff just got his driver's license two weeks ago. Neither of them is saying the obvious: *What if there's been an accident?*

It's 6:17 when the door opens. Both Sarah and Jim hurry into the living room to see Madison standing in the doorway.

Jim has his come-to-Jesus speech all prepared. But those words never have a chance.

(You're probably wishing you knew why Jim's speech got the kibosh. Well, again, as you wish.)

Several months before, a few days after a recent ugly exchange, Madison decided to Skype Allison.

"Grandma, it was bad. He did it again."

"Give me the details, Madison."

"He went off on me. In front of my friend and Mom and Aiden."

"I'm so sorry."

"I thought it was going to be different. But I don't know if much has really changed."

After listening to Madison a little longer, Allison responded, "Honey, I've got an idea. You can tell me no if you want. Grab a pen and some paper, will you?"

"Give me a second. I'll be right back."

Madison got up for a moment and then re-entered the picture with a notepad and pen.

"All right, now I'm just making this up as I go. But let's try this. When we get off this call, I want you to ask your dad to figure out an evening you both have free this next week. First thing you do that evening is to drive through a fast food place and grab something for the ride. You're gonna be out there for a while. You get to pick the food. Write that down.

"No music. No radio. No nothing. I think the town is Apache Junction. Is there an Apache Junction out there?"

"Yep, way out in the desert."

"Perfect. Write that down. Tell him the two of you are going to drive out there and back. And let your dad know that I'm the one who gave you this idea. If this goes south, he'll have his mom to deal with."

"Got it."

"Now, write this down. I want you to ask each other this question: 'What one thing could I do to help earn your trust?' Except he has to ask, 'What three things could I do?' Are you getting this?"

"I think I've got it, grandma. One for me, three for Dad."

"Oh, yes. This next question is just for you to think about. Would your dad earn some trust if just once he let you protect him before he exploded?"

"What do you mean, 'protect him'?"

"If just once, he believed that you would back off if he didn't lose his temper. If just once you had a way to stop him, and he'd let you."

"I don't see that happening."

"But what if there was a way to give your dad an exit ramp in the very moments before he flipped out?"

"I don't know, Grandma."

"Humor me. What would happen next, Madison? If your dad let you stop him just before the explosion?"

"Well, I guess I wouldn't get all up in his face."

"And then?"

"And then, well, maybe he wouldn't start preaching. I don't actually know. It never gets that far."

"Okay. So what if there was a code?"

"What?"

"A code. An agreed-upon phrase."

This code would be a way for Madison to let her dad know she was not trying to challenge or play him. That he could stand down, with a promise they would talk about it the moment they could get out of the public setting where embarrassment can ramp up the ugliness. The phrase would be a way to stop him before his spooled-up tornado cut a swath through her heart.

"Why don't you try suggesting that on the drive with your dad?"

And so she did. As they made the turn back on Highway 60 near Apache Junction, Madison explained to her dad what Allison suggested.

"So you'd use the phrase at the moment you're convinced that I'm about to lose it on you? Is that what you're saying?"

"I think so."

"I'd have to believe that you weren't just working me in order to get out of trouble."

"You'd have to trust me, Dad."

"Okay, what phrase were you thinking?"

Madison tried out several. The atmosphere in the car lightened as they both laughed at the absurdity of the whole thing.

Then she picked one out. He liked it. They each laughed again at the thought of her ever actually using the phrase.

In that moment, they were both filled with a sense of something they'd not experienced before. Jim was choosing, or at least promising to choose, to let his own daughter protect him, not excuse him, in the moment of his most unprotected area of his life. They were still smiling as they walked in the door that evening.

> "Protection happens when I encounter God's protective love in a trusted other who I ask to access my life in exchange for their protection."

And all of heaven waits to see if this can happen in real time, for Jim.

Now, months later, Madison has yet to try out the grand experiment. Jim has actually forgotten the phrase. Mostly it was just a good reminder that the two of them cared enough to even think of such a thing.

But now that the moment is here, it will take a lot of courage for Madison to try it. She has been rehearsing this scene for the last forty-five minutes, from the moment she knew she would be late.

What if he blows her off? What if he overrides his commitment to stand down? What if he throws it back in her face? There is a lot on the line with the next several moments.

And then a fifteen-year-old girl gives trust a chance.

"Dad, I really like your haircut."

Oblivious in his prepared anger, Jim spits back, "I didn't get a haircut!"

Just before he is about to lose it, she smiles at him and tries again, a bit more slowly. "I said, Dad, I really do like your haircut."

And then, in the time it takes to breathe, it hits him.

To stop a triggered temper explosion in Jim is like stopping a golf swing on the descent. But in this moment, something stronger is revealed. His daughter is taking the supreme gamble that her father, if given the chance, could be trusted with her heart. And so a destructive generational pattern is, in a breath, dealt a severe blow. Jim Clawson allows his daughter to protect him.

In mid-breath, Jim stops.

Sarah doesn't understand what is happening. Nor does the next person stepping into the house.

That would be Jeff.

"Mr. Clawson, please let me explain!"

Everything is moving in slow motion for Jim. He responds, still in shock, "Yes, Jeff, I would like that."

"Mr. and Mrs. Clawson. This is all on me. We took a hike out in the preserve. I was the one who said we should leave our phones at home. I know. Stupid. I still have no idea why I said that. Anyway, we lost track of time. By the time I asked a hiker what time it was, we were already late and a mile from the car. I'm so sorry. Madison kept telling me earlier we should get back. Mr. and Mrs. Clawson, I really screwed up here."

Sarah breaks the silence. "There's plenty of lasagna left. Stay for dinner, Jeff."

"Thank you, Mrs. Clawson. But I'm pretty sure I'm in trouble at my home too."

Jim has all sorts of things he wants to say to Jeff in this moment. The only words he can get out are, "Thank you for being straight with me, Jeff. I believe you."

Jeff waves 'bye to Madison, then turns and hurries out the door.

Jim also has all sorts of things he wants to say to Madison in this moment. The only words he can get out are, "Thank you, Madison."

"You're welcome, Dad. Sorry I scared you both."

Sarah directs Madison toward lasagna. Jim finds something to do in the garage. And Sarah pretends to read a magazine, sitting not far from Madison.

By the time Aiden is dropped off later, Jim, Sarah, and Madison have all settled into getting ready for bed. There will be no talks tonight. They will laugh and retell this story about the haircut line many times in the future. But tonight, it's all too fresh. None of them are yet even certain what has really taken place.

But Madison, in front of the mirror, combing her hair, whispers these words: "Thanks, Grandma."

Seven months ago, this family was drifting away from each other and didn't know why or how to find their way back. They were learning a pattern of pulling away.

And God showed up. He has shown up before. He was there all along. And He will have to dramatically show up again—often.

For this is not a once-and-for-all, triumphant, happy Hallmark ending. Such stories are not to be trusted. They do not exist, except in movies.

The Clawsons will still hurt each other. Jim will strain the goodness accomplished this evening not so many weeks from now. Madison will fail in her choices more than once. Sarah will periodically see her mom's performance doctrine in her own parenting. And Aiden. Well, Aiden will continue to be Aiden. Only with even more eclectic clothing decisions.

But the course of this family has been irrevocably changed. God has intervened in His astonishing grace.

In spite of their clumsiness and failures, Jim and Sarah are slowly earning the trust of Madison and Aiden.

Jim and Sarah are learning to enjoy the ride.

REFLECTION QUESTIONS

What follows are two questions/reflections for each episode except the last one. For that episode, there's just one thing to consider (and it's rather big). Our hope is that you'll read through these questions and consider your responses. If you're a couple, there's a ton of benefit in working through these together. Or maybe separately, then coming together to discuss. (Yeah, that's better, huh?) But this book and these questions could also be used in a gathering of parents (married couples, single parents, grandparents). Warning—such a gathering might get messy and real and beautiful.

EPISODE 1: MEET THE PARENTS

1. As we meet Jim and Sarah, we're also meeting ourselves in a sense, right? Parents are parents; families are families. The details may be different but the generalities are common to us all. Pick and underline a few lines in the story where, when you read them, you thought, *I've been there before.*

2. For those lines where you thought, *I've been there a dozen times!* That may be a clue into an unresolved issue you're carrying. That issue comes from your wounding. Remember, unless your wounding is identified and addressed so it can be redeemed and healed, you will remain with an unresolved issue. And your children will be stunted in their immaturity by this.

EPISODE 2: UNDER NEW MANAGEMENT

1. Take a minute and focus on your kids. Can you see them? Okay, good. Now really focus. If you had to vote between the two, are they compliant or rebellious? What other words help describe your thoughts?

2. Now take a minute and focus on yourself. It's fine; the selfish police are not here right now, so don't worry. Can you see yourself? What five words would you use to describe yourself right now as a parent? We'll get you started with a suggestion—exhausted. Right? Choose five more, and be honest. Go.

- _____

- _____

- _____

- _____

- _____

EPISODE 3: A MATTER OF TRUST

1. "As a parent, there is nothing more important than earning your children's trust." Do you believe that statement? If you do, why do you believe it? Back up your belief. If you don't believe that, what do you believe is the most important thing in relation to your children? What do you have to back that up?

2. How would your children grade you in terms of trust? What letter grade would you receive? Think traditional school grades: A, B, C, D, and F. A = my parents are trustworthy, while F = I trust my parents as far as I can throw them.

EPISODE 4: YESTERDAY IS GONE

1. Our parents. Our mom and dad. Whether they were superstars or lazybones or something in between, they were/are the tallest trees in our forest. And whether we like it or not, we absorb some of their parenting patterns. It's inevitable. Name one of those parenting patterns. Is that a good pattern? Or do you hate it when you catch yourself parenting that way?

2. Hang on, super important question here. Do you know you are completely righteous and holy, right now? Not just some day, after enough strenuous diligence and endless performance. But right now? If you answered yes, where did that belief come from? Your family? Your church? Did you discover that in some book? But if you answered no, what about that statement seems off a little or possibly gives you pause?

EPISODE 5: A TASTE OF DISCIPLINE

1. This episode talked about parenting tastes versus parenting right and wrong, and the difference between the two. Think about most of the conflicts you have with your children. Are most of them taste related? And yes, by "taste" we mean different than yours.

2. Discipline is always for the benefit of the one receiving the discipline. Discipline should be thoughtful and intentional. Can you think of an example when this was not true of your approach with your child? Looking back, how could you have approached that differently?

EPISODE 6: THE HEART OF THE MATTER

1. You heard Jim affirm his mom in front of Sarah and the kids. Is there someone in your life you can point to, someone like Allison, who kept loving you and believing in you regardless of your response at the time? What would it look like for you to affirm that person? A handwritten letter? A speech in front of family or friends? A phone call?

2. Now consider someone on the opposite end of the spectrum, someone like Jim's dad, Ray, that you'd like to give a swift boot to their backside. Chances are really good that forgiveness is the name of the game with that person. Chances are just as good that you're acting as judge and jury in relation to that person. Remember, there is an order to forgiveness: first vertical, then horizontal. In that order. What would it look like to follow that order and move toward that person in love?

EPISODE 7: THE ROAD TO MY HEART

1. Permission to the heart is earned. What do you think? Is that just something those crazy people who live in the desert believe? Or is there truth there? Think about that in relation to your children. If you believe that statement, what are you doing or not doing to earn their trust? Try to be precise here.

2. Sarah and Allison engaged in a significant conversation at Dori's Tea Cottage. They covered a lot of ground. Look back at their conversation. What was one thing Allison said (there were probably more, but choose one) that got your attention? It may have grabbed your attention because it sounded so true. Or it may have given you pause because you're not quite sure you understand it.

EPISODE 8: WHEN YOU BUILD ME UP

1. Reflect on the community you were raised in; if it was a faith community consider that too. How was affirmation handled? Was it handed out sparingly, because pride cometh before a fall? Or was it dispensed with generosity, openhandedly, joyfully? Or was it some strange combination of the two, depending on the personalities involved?

2. Feeling risky? Aw, c'mon, why not? How about trying Sarah's affirmation exercise, the one she initiated with her family? All you need are pens, paper, and three positive thoughts about the people in your family. And after the affirming is done, the affirmed can respond with how it made them feel. Now don't expect it to go like it did in this episode. It might, although it might not. But the point is that you risked trusting and being trusted.

EPISODE 9: IN THE RING WITH THE BULLS OF REALITY

1. Are you afraid to let your kids in on your poor choices from the past? This is usually a yes or no question—not much space for gray here. Maybe the thought of that scares you to death because you pulled some doozies. Can you see that

being vulnerable with your children is actually a protective measure? Why, or why not?

2. Wouldn't it have been nice for this story to end after the experiences at Convict Lake? No big red bows, but everybody felt better, closer. But that didn't happen, and Jim and Sarah found themselves on a battlefield of epic proportions. And as brutal as that confrontation was (and it was), something was different when the smoke cleared, something messy but beautiful. Choose a couple of words to describe how you felt at the conclusion of this episode. Yes, this is a feely question, and even if you don't like feely questions, we believe you can handle just this one.

EPISODE 10: SOMEONE TO WATCH OVER ME

1. In an age-appropriate way, ask your child this question: "What one thing could I do to help earn your trust?" And then be okay with whatever they tell you. Trust the God who created you to be the mom or the dad. And start enjoying the ride, because goodness, it goes fast. Trust us.

If you've been touched by the imaginative freedom of this story and want to help make it available to others at a wider level, we invite you to participate in...

THE CURE & PARENTS PROJECT

Word of mouth is still the most effective tool for a book like this to gain a hearing in the culture.

Give the book to friends, even acquaintances, as a gift. They will not only experience an exhilarating journey but also get a glimpse of the true face of God.

To order, go to Amazon.com. When ordering multiple copies, go to trueface.org and look for bulk discounts. *The Cure and Parents* is also available on all ebook formats, including Kindle, and as an audio book.

Please feel free to leave us a review on Amazon, or if you have a Facebook page, blog, or website, consider sharing about the book, without giving away the story.

If you own a shop or business, consider putting a display of *The Cure and Parents* on your counter to resell to customers. Or buy a set of books for prisons or rehabilitations homes where people can discover hope and joy in *The Cure and Parents.*

Follow us on Instagram: @truefacelife
Follow us on Twitter: @truefaced
"Like" our Facebook page: facebook.com/truefacecommunity
Small Group & Churchwide Series resource available at trueface.org

Thank you for being a carrier of the cure with us,

John & Stacey
Bruce & Janet
Bill & Grace

ACKNOWLEDGMENTS

Writing a book on parenting is not like writing a book on the future of plutonium. With a parenting book, individuals can comment from experience whether or not you know what you're talking about. Like your own kids, for example.

They each have had to experience our failures in the very truths we are asking you to consider. This would all be just theory and bluffing if our children hadn't trusted God and given us permission to become parents who could earn their trust.

Bill and Grace thank Bill, Wende, and Joy. John and Stacey thank Caleb, Amy, and Carly. Bruce and Janet thank Nicole, Chad, and Ryan.

There are not enough words to thank each of you.

All six of us co-authors are honored to give great thanks to these following friends.

Through the years, many of you strongly implored us to write a book on grace-based parenting. Now, many of your children have their own children! Thanks to each of you for spurring us on so that many parents finally have this book in their hands.

Over fifty parents also invested their time reading draft manuscripts, making vital suggestions that enriched the clarity and flow. We know who you are, and we thank you.

We do not have enough room in this book to adequately express our thanks to our board members, advisory council, and friends of Trueface. All of them are our dear, committed friends. They, along with their families, have sacrificed significantly. From resources to schedules, they have stood arm in arm with us in this message of God's redemption, grace, and destiny. They continually encourage, protect, and pray for us. They also direct us in learning how to get this ancient message to the world.

The dedicated staff of Trueface has believed and lived out the truths of new life in Christ. They are not simply employees, but passionate and skilled servants, committed to risk this life we are promising. If you drop by our main office in Phoenix or any of the scattered places where our staff and faculty serve, you will experience the very real, messy, beautiful, and authentic markings of an environment of grace. Thank you, fellow team members.

The team at CrossSection (CrossSection.com) because they deeply believe in the message and life we are sharing. Then there are the many businesses, foundations, institutions, ministries, and churches, including Open Door Fellowship, who continue to heroically hold to this grand experiment of grace and identity in Christ.

For some time, we have been watching and admiring John Blase's editing (thebeautifuldue.wordpress.com). Now we have the privilege of getting to work with him. John has helped draw out the tone, clarity, and conciseness he knew we wanted. It is uncommon to find a creative editor who shares a way of seeing and theology the way he does with us. John has been of immense help to this book. Matt Johnson has also contributed his talents to the editing of this book.

Linda Harris (perfectwordediting.com) has once again artfully and copiously combed through our words to catch the inconsistencies, typos, grammar issues and general lack of real English.

David and Kelsie Pinkerton wrote the foreword for this book. We also trusted them to help us accurately see the story through the eyes of thirty-something-year-old parents. The four couples, ranging from their thirties to seventies, trusted each other, submitted to each other, and laughed together so hard it should be illegal. David and Kelsie will be carrying this message forward long after some of us are eating pie in the land without need of light.

Oh, by the way, the three couples—Bill and Grace, John and Stacey, and Bruce and Janet—still love, respect, and protect each other with our entire hearts. The relational waters are not always smooth, as we three couples create a team of very different and strong personalities. God has kept His hand on us these last twenty-some years. He has taught us how we can flourish together in committed relationships of love, experiencing the kind of undeserved and incredible community you read about in *The Cure*.

ABOUT THE AUTHORS

BILL & GRACE THRALL

As a young CPA and the first Assistant Auditor General of Arizona, Bill and Grace left business to establish Open Door Fellowship. The Thralls pastored there for over 25 years. This faith community became a regional influence for nurturing many young leaders and their ministries. For example, Neighborhood Ministries was birthed from this community and Bill served on the founding Boards of Frontiers and Christian Family Care. Bill and Grace's learnings have been penned throughout *The Cure, The Ascent of a Leader, Bo's Café, Behind the Mask,* and *High Trust Cultures.* Bill is particularly gifted in helping leaders establish trust in all their key relationships, from CEOs of international companies to heads of mission organizations and universities. Bill and Grace have three grown children: Bill married to Charlotte, Wende married to Jim, and Joy married to Joe. This has, so far, produced nine grandchildren and one great-grandchild. Bill and Grace have hosted thousands in their home, while Bill takes every chance he gets to create beautiful wood furniture and go golfing or fly-fishing with his family and friends.

JOHN & STACEY LYNCH

John and Stacey raised their family in Phoenix, Arizona, where John served as teaching pastor of Open Door Fellowship for 27 years. The authenticity, longevity, and playfulness of these two communities, Open Door and Trueface, bring real-world reality and potency to the message of Trueface. In addition to speaking extensively with the Trueface team, John is a best-selling co-author of *The Cure, Bo's Café, Behind the Mask,* and his own story, *On My Worst Day.* John also powerfully delivered the classic "Two Roads Two Rooms" allegory, which the three co-authors created for *The Cure.* This talk can be viewed or listened to on various social media outlets. Stacey, too, carries a gift for communication and has served hundreds of families and children as a speech pathologist. John and Stacey often create embracing environments for people to enjoy authentic community on their backyard patio and elsewhere. They are passionate parents to their three children: Caleb married to Kali, with granddaughters Maci and Payton; Amy married to Cody, with grandchildren Ridge and Navy; and Carly.

BRUCE & JANET McNICOL

In 1995, the McNicols moved from Chicago to Phoenix to start Trueface, with the Thralls, where Bruce has served as President for 21 years. Bruce and Janet, enriched by her nursing career, thrive on walking alongside leaders across the spectrum of health care and the professions of entertainment, sports, government, and the church, opening pathways for these leaders to experience the healing and freedom of the original good news. God has used the McNicols' leadership to help Trueface offer epiphanies of grace for many thousands around the world. With degrees in finance, law, theology, leadership and organizational development, Bruce's gifting to teach and write to diverse audiences has proved true in the 4.5+ Amazon ratings of the books he has co-authored: *The Cure, The Ascent of a Leader, Bo's Café, Behind the Mask,* and others. Bruce and Janet have received life-changing tutoring from their three wonderful children and spouses: Nicole, married to Kory, with grandchildren Willo and Elliott; Chad married to Erica; and Ryan. When time affords, the McNicols love to address international cultural needs, mentor young leaders and couples, and enjoy hiking, reading, travel, sports, comedy, and the arts.

THE TRUEFACE MISSION

TRUEFACE.ORG - CARRIERS OF THE CURE

Trueface is part of a global movement to see millions of high-trust communities of grace multiplied around the world. Because we believe Grace Changes Everything!

Grace changes how we read the Bible and trust its truths. Grace changes how we see the true face of Jesus and our desire to follow Him. Grace changes how we heal, mature, and live out the dreams God has for us. Grace alters how we create a safe environment in our marriages, families, and friendships.

Grace changes how we resolve prejudice, discrimination, and oppression. Grace changes how we handle conflict, sin, anger, addiction, shame, and failure. Grace changes how we forgive, repent, and develop emotionally healthy relationships.

Grace changes how we teach, motivate, disciple, and inspire our faith communities. Most importantly, grace changes how we see God, ourselves, and others.

Grace changes everything!

To help restore this original good news for you, Trueface offers a variety of means for your journey, including books, study guides, events, retreats, videos, podcasts, social media, group online education, consulting and partnerships. In this relational process, we believe you may discover the true face of Jesus, again—maybe for the first time. He is the Source of every high-trust community of grace.

CONTACT US AT INFO@TRUEFACE.ORG

Enjoy the ride

Whether we are reacting to our parents, planning to be parents, overwhelmed at being parents, or learning to stand with our kids as they now parent, we need to know there is a way home. A way to be convinced God is in the middle of every stage of our family. It always begins with us, the parents, and will always involve us working to earn our children's trust.

This book is filled with hope, joy, insight, wisdom and maybe a fresh way of seeing. We get to ride with a family as they struggle through the same mistakes we can make. Then we watch them imperfectly, but wonderfully learn to find each other.

"As young parents, we feel like we've been given a cheat book on parenting, not only for our kids—but for our own hearts."
Jason & Garyfalia Pamer, Executive Producers *The Heart of Man*

"The Cure & Parents offers a critically important truth and practical steps to live it out. As a parent of three boys I recommend it."
Danielle Strickland, Ambassador, Compassion International
Author, *The Ultimate Exodus: Finding Freedom From What Enslaves You*

"Honest, practical, and full of grace... everyone should read this book."
Jeremy & Larisa Affeldt, Retired Major League Pitcher & World Series Champion

$14.99
ISBN 978-1-934104-09-5
51499>

TRUEFACE
trueface.org

9 781934 104095

LEVEL TWO

Truck

An all-new story from the *New York Times* bestselling creators of *Click, Clack, Moo: Cows That Type*

doreen cronin and betsy lewin

Ready to read?

THEN REACH FOR THE STARS!

Each child is a rising star in our Ready-to-Read program, gaining confidence as they launch from one reading level to the next. With a constellation of engaging, soon-to-be favorite stories and starring characters to lead the way, we encourage beginning readers to enjoy the journey of learning to read.

The Ready-to-Read stories are grouped into five reading levels:

READY-TO-GO! ★ STELLAR STARTER!
Stories created for the very new reader, using sight words, word families, and rhythm, rhyme, and repetition.

PRE-LEVEL ONE ★ RISING STAR READER!
Stories are shared reading experiences, featuring familiar characters and simple words.

LEVEL ONE ★ STAR READER!
Stories feature easy sight words and words to sound out, simple plot and dialogue, as well as familiar topics and themes.

LEVEL TWO ★ SUPERSTAR READER!
Stories have simple chapters, longer sentences, and high-interest vocabulary words.

LEVEL THREE ★ MEGASTAR READER!
Stories have longer, more complex plots and character development, challenging vocabulary words, and more difficult sentence structure.

Confidence is a big key to learning to read, and whether a child is a Stellar Starter or a Megastar, this program is designed to help kids feel like stars at **every** reading level. With the help of their favorite characters, every reading star will sparkle and shine as they take pride in their abilities and learn to love reading.

Blast off on this starry adventure . . . a universe of reading awaits!